Praise for

I met Sharon when my son was just over three years old. She was his case manager, part of the child study team along with, John Lestino, child psychologist. At the time, my son was listed as multiple disabled; the Autism label followed. This was uncharted territory for our family. It was a time of uncertainty and heartache. As I worked with Sharon over the years, she became family. I could call her at anytime, day or night. She would always answer her phone with encouragement, ideas, or just to lend an ear. She shared stories of past students like my son and gave me HOPE when we were lost navigating the Autism world. We collaborated on ideas, we discussed issues and ways to overcome those issues, and we also shared our son's triumphs. She always had ideas she drew on from her past experience, thinking outside the box if that's what it took. She moved mountains to make things happen.

At graduation, she sat in the front row, shedding tears of joy for Johnny achievements. She watched a little boy who was lost and communicate blossom into a boy who could sing in a choir and tell her " Hi Mrs. Cohen," every time he saw her. My son, has overcome so many obstacles in his life. Obstacles that Sharon and John removed so he could succeed !

Christine Boucouvalas
Parent

Sharon Benaderet-Cohen, provides the reader with multiple examples of how she has inspired others to "Touch a Life". Mrs. Cohen skillfully guides the audience through a series of events that shaped her role as a teacher and mentor. Her real life examples demonstrate to others how to overcome barriers that initially seem impenetrable. The families often struggle to accept their child's disability and Mrs. Cohen describes how she and her colleagues brainstormed solutions that ultimately resulted in matching services to enhance the child's academic and emotional success.

Suzanne R. Cote MA, NASP, LMFC
Adjunct Professor Rowan University

As an education professional working with future classroom teachers, this is exactly the type of book that I would recommend pre-service teachers add to their personal library. Sharon drives home a very important message and helps future teachers understand how to look at their kids as individuals and find the "good" in all. The anecdotal stories help illustrate each chapter's message in an authentic way and really gets to the "heart" of what it means to be a great teacher. I am very proud of Sharon's first book and look forward to her adding more to the field.

Dr. Kay Burks
Assistant Professor of Education & Coordinator of Teacher Education
University of South Carolina Aiken

Sharon Cohen is a dedicated and consummate teacher who has dedicated decades to educating young students and future teachers. Through the examples and stories she presents in this book, Sharon shares the wisdom of her extensive experience to inform and guide future teachers as they begin their own journey in educating others.

Frances M. Sessa, Ph.D.
Division Head, Social Sciences
Associate Professor, Psychology
Penn State University-Abington

Touch a
Life

Inspirational Stories on Teaching
to the Good in *All* Types of Students

A Guide for Teachers, Student Teachers & Parents

Sharon Benaderet-Cohen, M.Ed., LDT/C

Dear Ruth,
If you dream it, you can do it!
Love,
Sharon

Touch a Life
Inspirational Stories on Teaching
to the Good in All Types of Students

By Sharon Benaderet-Cohen, M.Ed., LDT/C
Copyright©2018

ISBN: 978-0-692-14723-8

All rights reserved
Printed in the United States of America

No part of this book may be used or reproduced in any manner whatsoever without the written permission of the author except in the case of brief quotations embodied in critical articles and reviews.

The names in this book have been changed to protect the confidentiality of the students and parents.

Published by Sharon Benaderet-Cohen, M.Ed., LDT/C

Cover Design: Eric Labacz, www.labaczdesign.com

I dedicate my book to my husband of 46 years for believing in me and observing these successes throughout the years. Also, my deepest gratitude goes to my two daughters, Edie and Dana, for their inspiration and support. Special thanks to my sister Abby for continuing to be the wind beneath my wings.

A child is like a butterfly in the wind.
Some can fly higher than others.
But each one flies the best that it can.
Why compare one against the other?
Each one is different.
Each one is special.
Each one is beautiful.

Anonymous

    This poem hung in my office because it reminded me of my own personal philosophy of education. This book is a collection of inspiring stories of how to find the "good" in each child, and teach to that good. It teaches you how to "Touch a Life" and have them touch yours. Teaching is more than an art. It is a way of working with mutual communication. No matter how challenging a student may be, treating him or her with love, kindness, and respect will make them soar to new heights. In my 44-year career as an educator, I have found so many ways that my students touched my life in a positive way. I also have inspired their lives in positive ways.

    As an educator, my vast career covers many types of education. These include teaching regular education, special education, being a Learning Disabilities/Teacher Consultant, an Adjunct College Professor, and a Supervisor of Student Teachers. In each of my positions I have been inspired by my students to reach for the highest heights. They, in turn, have "touched' mine in return. This book is dedicated to them for being an inspiration to us all!

Contents

Foreword 1
Introduction 3
Chapter 1: Dedication 5
Chapter 2: Dignity 18
Chapter 3: Trust 23
Chapter 4: Kindness 30
Chapter 5: Positivity 36
Chapter 6: Forgiveness 44
Chapter 7: Empathy 50
Chapter 8: Love 58
Chapter 9: Celebrate 64
Chapter 10: Compassion 72
Chapter 11: Equality 81
Chapter 12: Confidence 87
Chapter 13: Enthusiasm 91
Chapter 14: Inspire 98
Chapter 15: Gratitude 105
Chapter 16: Win-Win 113
Conclusion 117
Acknowledgments 120
About the Author 121

Foreword

It has officially been two-and-a-half years since my life was touched in the most beautiful way. Recalling my first time meeting Professor Cohen at Penn State Abington in the late summer of 2015, I had no idea the level of impact that she would soon play in my life. Upon hearing her introduce herself to our cohort of incoming student teachers, I remember listening in awe and amazement as she recalled her own experiences during her extensive career in education. Upon hearing that she would be my student-teaching supervisor, I was elated, knowing that I would be coached by the very best in the field.

Mrs. Cohen has the magical ability of connecting with all of her students on a different level. She is an incredible mentor to every student because she recognizes each individual's strength and is able to capitalize on it. She provides love and encouragement while having very high expectations for her students, which are all traits of an ideal educator.

Touch a Life focuses on Mrs. Cohen's incredible, 44-year career in education, along with heart-warming stories of significant students whose lives she has touched along the way. This book serves as an ideal resource for students, parents,and anyone in the education field who aspires to work with diverse learners, of all ages and of all stages.

Having been coached and mentored by such a brilliant educator, I felt extremely prepared to begin my own career as a teacher. Today, our picture together sits atop my desk in my very own classroom, serving as a constant reminder of the woman who believed in me from the very beginning. As I look into the smiling faces of my 24 second grade students, all with diverse academic abilities, I think about Mrs. Cohen's words to me: "Each child has a gift. Find the talents and abilities in every child and teach to those strengths." The wisdom she passed on to me is now indirectly passed to every child that I teach. She will always be a constant presence in my classroom.

I consider myself extremely lucky to have been educated by Professor Cohen at the collegiate level, but for those who aspire to be just as brilliant in the field, *Touch a Life* will serve as a great resource to teach and inspire.

Mrs. Cohen has been a coach, a mentor, a professor and most importantly, a loving friend. I recognize that very few people have someone who has played so many significant roles in their lives and have personally inspired them. Mrs. Cohen not only touched my life. She changed it. Forever.

Katelyn Scott

Introduction

After graduating from Penn State in 1972, I thought that sealed my destiny—to teach elementary school forever. I taught fifth grade for three years. However, I was drawn to the class that we passed on the way to lunch in the basement of my school. That was the class for difficult students, otherwise known as special education.

It was then that I discovered my passion for students who were more challenging. Back to school I went, this time to get my Master's Degree in Special Education. Year after year, placement after placement, I was assigned to teach the difficult students. I thoroughly enjoyed every single class and the new challenges that they brought.

After 21 years of teaching I turned my talents to a new position. I went back to graduate school for a certificate as a Learning Disabilities Teacher/Consultant. My new career drew upon my classroom experience. But now I worked with teachers and their students. My love for education took a new turn.

I retired after 41 years, and after only one year I knew I

needed something to stimulate my brain. My decision came to re-invent myself once again, and this time I became an adjunct professor at Penn State Abington. Now my students were in college. After writing my course and teaching it, I fell in love with teaching 22-year-olds. My class evolved into supervising student teachers. Passion and inspiration took over, and I continued to love my work every day. It was thrilling to watch these young students to evolve into outstanding teachers.

Last year on graduation day I stood in the campus auditorium in full regalia. My career came full circle; 49 years ago, I began my educational path at this very campus. My path did not only lead me in many directions. My passion helped many, many students find their "good."

This book was born during my days at Penn State. In order to make my course meaningful, I told these inspirational stories. At the end of each chapter is a page for you to take notes on any ideas that you can use. My students loved hearing my stories. I always told them they have the power to "Touch a Life" and, in turn, have students touch theirs. Hence, the birth of *Touch a Life*. Let me lead you to my passion!

Chapter 1
Dedication

In a teacher's career if you are lucky enough to teach a student on the Autism Spectrum, you will automatically know the meaning of dedication. These two inspirational stories of very different students were the impetus for writing my book. The first boy touched my life in a very special way while I was a Learning Consultant and the second one was when I was a special education teacher. They were very different but each inspired me to become a better educator.

Jimmie

It was a beautiful morning when John, my co-worker and partner, and I were assigned to test a two-and-a-half-year-old boy. His mother, a woman with a beautiful smile and cheery attitude, opened the door and a little boy hid behind her. We all went into her living room to talk. Jimmie never made eye contact, nor did he utter one word. He had John crawling all over the living room attempting to get him to respond. Jimmie walked to the backyard and engaged with all of the equipment out there, but there was no interaction with my partner. Kristen, his mother, told us that her husband was an avid golfer, and little Jimmie had his own set of golf clubs. We all went upstairs to look at them. Jimmie played with them, but still no eye contact or interaction with us. Finally, we all went into the kitchen to sit down and talk. There was a box of munchkins on top of the microwave. Jimmie moved a chair and placed it right in front of the counter and microwave. He took some munchkins out of the box and then carefully put the chair back. He then enjoyed eating his munchkins. Wow! With no apparent communication skills he was able to problem solve. This was his greatest asset. After a two-hour visit of pure observational data and background information from his mother, John and I were able to obtain enough information to write a thorough report.

  About one month later we met with both of Jimmie's parents to review our report. Our findings were to classify Jimmie multiply disabled with suspicions of Autism; however, a doctor needed to make that official call. We discussed the lack of eye contact and language, but highlighted Jimmie's problem solving skills. His father was of Greek decent and sat at a distance from us. He asked us when he would be able to have a conversation with his son. This was very important to him. We believed that in his culture, he could not accept a son who was not perfect. Kristen, on the other hand, was just happy to hear we could provide services for her son. I got up and went back to my office to get a letter that was written to me by a former parent. It contained 12 pages of all the ways I helped her son while he was in my charge. Kristen had tears flowing down her cheeks as she listened to all of the strengths this other little boy developed in my class. She looked at her husband and said, "Honey, Sharon is giving us hope." They agreed to place Jimmie in a very small class in special education, which would address all his needs.

Many different placements occurred for Jimmie while in elementary school. By that time, his doctor had officially diagnosed him as Autistic. One of my biggest regrets as an educator at that time was being unable to develop a support system for parents who had gone through the process and come out on the other end. They could be there to help the parents who were presently going through it. Due to lack of time with my responsibilities, I never did develop this support system. This was the early 2000s and there were no concrete support systems for parents of Autistic children.

A breakthrough came when Jimmie was about to enter our middle school. Our school district was forming an Autistic class in the fall. My partner John and I were not too apprehensive because all our elementary schools were familiar with Autism and we had developed a very special program called "Reverse Inclusion." We asked for volunteer regular education fourth grade students whose parents would allow them to work in our preschool Autistic classes. They were assigned a peer buddy and a partner to work with. These students not only helped the Autistic students with academics, but they worked with them on social skills also. It was remarkable watching them play miniature basketball hoops in the hallway, or games designed to develop interaction. The older students were touched as they inspired our smaller Autistic students to develop. This program did so much for increasing self-esteem on the part of both the Autistic students and the helpers. It also taught our older students not to fear students who were different from them. They could walk through a mall and not feel the need to stare at anyone because of their differences. Also if a student had a meltdown in the hallway, they understood how to handle it. It was a win-win situation all the way around. We could never figure out which student got more out of this special relationship, but we knew this program we had developed really worked!

Jimmie's principal and vice principal decided to be proactive with Jimmie and the other students' arrival. It was still summer, and they had time to plan for the arrival of this "special" class. We sat and brainstormed at a meeting with Kristen. Together, we came up with the idea of showing the entire school audience and faculty the Temple Grandin movie. They all watched together at the assembly, and they all seemed to appreciate the trials and triumphs of this brave young woman who lives with Autism. She has achieved a Ph. D. and is an example that you can achieve anything you set your mind to. The class was officially moved into the building, and Jimmie became part of the sixth grade class. He became so well liked that it gave me goose bumps when I attended the basketball game between the faculty and the students. Jimmie was a wonderful athlete. When he ran to throw a basketball into the net, the entire gym cheered "Go, Jimmie, go." They embraced him because he was a kind, lovable human being, not because he was different.

One morning I was walking down the hall to attend a meeting, and I passed Jimmie. He was the messenger taking the lunch count down to the office. He made eye contact with me and said, "Good morning, Mrs. Cohen." I got chills down my spine from this small miracle. My, he had come such a far cry from the first time I set eyes on him. He had made academic progress, but moreover, he had made friends and was accepted by his peers.

Toward the second half of eighth grade, two more miraculous things happened. Kristen came in for an IEP meeting. That is an Individual Education Plan for special education students. She mentioned how Jimmie loved to sing in the shower and that he knew all of the words to all of the songs the chorus sang in the school's holiday show. We looked at each other and had the same thought: What about getting Jimmie into the chorus for the Spring

Concert. After our meeting I asked our music teacher if that could become a possibility. He was very big into inclusion and said "Sure, as long as Kristen is willing to review the words with him, and she must stay with him for rehearsals."

Kristen was on cloud nine when I called her with the good news. Her Jimmie was receiving normalcy once again. It had also become a triumph for our school. We were looking for Jimmie's "good" and teaching to it.

The icing on the cake was when I entered the building one morning and walked past the lunchroom. I saw Jimmie with a green apron that matched the lunchroom ladies. He had a ladle in his hands and was doling peaches into little cups. The ladies loved Jimmie and knew he loved repetitive things. His parents owned a Wawa store and Jimmie had a job there. His favorite duty job was putting the gallons of milk on the shelves. Bingo, they came up with a way for vocational training in a traditional middle school. I still love these ladies to this day. They found Jimmie's "good," and they gave him a job to teach to that good.

The Grand Finale for Jimmie was eighth grade graduation. When Jimmie's name was called to come up and receive his diploma, the entire audience cheered for 10 minutes straight. My partner John, Kristen, and I could not hold back the tears. Jimmie had brought so much joy into our lives. He touched our lives as we touched him. That is what the educational process is all about. Find the "good" in a student and have them touch yours. That's what good teaching is all about!

The pinnacle of my career happened at a dinner given for me upon my retirement dinner after working in education for 41 years. My co-worker, partner, and "school husband" surprised me. He kept telling me he had a big surprise for me. I saw Kristen enter, and I began to cry. Thinking that she was my surprise, I gave her a hug.

But lo and behold her appearance was not the surprise. She was invited to give my testimonial speech. Kristen began by describing the day that John and I came to her house and crawled around with Jimmie. She told everyone that in her depths of despair and heartache I called her and shared many success stories with her. She acknowledged that I even called her on weekends to give her hope and inspiration. We laughed together and cried together. Her son went from echolalia to singing in the choir.

"You can't put a price on what we have," she said. She thanked me for laying the foundation of bricks for her son. She also thanked my family for sharing me with them. She even showed the picture I had given Jimmie that said "Congratulations, Jimmie. We did it! Love, Sharon and John."

I looked around the room, and there wasn't a dry eye in the house. My entire family had tears streaming down their cheeks. Kristen ended by saying my legacy would live on in the hundreds of students and families I had touched, that I would always have a special place in her heart, and that I was an official member of her family. On the way out of the door I bumped into my superintendent. She told me that she has attended many retirement dinners, but she had never been to one where a parent gave a testimonial speech. It was at that moment that I knew I had "touched a life" and one had touched me.

Jimmie and his family moved out of state, but we always keep in touch. I received his junior and senior prom pictures and have them proudly placed on a special shelf in my office. His family presently lives in Syracuse, New York, and he is 19 years old. He is a fine-looking young man. Kristen has told me so many wonderful things about his continuous education. Because he is in Special Education, he is entitled to stay in high school until the age of 21, when he will be able to graduate. The school system he is presently

Touch a Life

in gives him three years of vocational training. Each year is different. The ultimate goal is for him is to work in a hospital as a custodian with a salary and benefits. When Jimmie graduates at the age of 21, John and I plan to attend. I wouldn't miss it for the world!

Luke

It was the beginning of my new career after receiving my Master's in Special Education. My new job as a teacher of students with Communication Handicaps was so exciting. I even took a course in Sign Language at Katzenback School for the Deaf in case I had a student with those needs. Several days before the start of the school year in 1983, I received a phone call from the Learning Disabilities Teacher/Consultant with whom I was to work. My student's mother had requested a meeting with our Team to discuss her son. Mrs. B. expressed concerns about her son's behavior. When we arrived for the meeting, she stared at the back coat room and asked if we put some fencing around it so her son Luke would have some space to run back and forth since he had excessive energy. We explained that this was not possible since it was a public school, not a private school. She was very upset about our decision. I asked her to trust me and that I would do my very best to accommodate her son.

On the first day of school, Hedy, the speech therapist, and I greeted each student. Our desks were arranged in rows, and each student sat at their desk. One student who had Cerebral Palsy sat in his wheelchair with his one-on-one aide by his side. My excitement burst like a balloon when Luke began running around the room. Each of us took turns spotting him. I can honestly say after all of my years in the classroom, I have never had a student who displayed this much energy. He zoomed on the playground and was non-stop. I thought, "This child is beyond ADHD and is going to be my most challenging this year." My assistant paid another visit and the three of us had an emergency meeting. She pulled out a box of tiny red dots and explained she wanted us to draw a behavior chart to represent each subject we taught. We were to give three dots on each subject for Luke for appropriate behavior. After she left we decided to try it and give it a week's trial. This system was so tedious because we were constantly concentrating on Luke. However, we had seven other students to teach.

    Putting our heads together, we decided to try another idea. I used my creativity to design a game board that contained blocks for each academic area along with before and after school activities such as lunch, specials, and recess. Each student received a new gameboard to play each day. We used Bingo dabbers to dab each block for good behavior. I also used a marble jar as a classroom management tool. Whenever I caught a student being "good" I dropped a marble in a jar so they could associate it with appropriate behavior. Luke began to buy into this system and sat for longer periods of time. Now the thing that still drove me crazy was his constant tapping on the desk as I was teaching. We sat at a kidney-shaped table with three or four students to teach reading. His insidious tapping was as nerve-wracking as fingernails on a chalkboard. My principal was observing one morning, and she watched Luke's fingers doing their tapping. She nonchalantly reached over and placed her hand on his, and the tapping stopped. Ms. Green had an extensive background as a reading specialist, so I thought I would give her idea a try. The only problem with me doing it was when I had to constantly lean over and put my hands on his. After about a month of frustration, I thought I would try something novel. I remembered in one of my special ed classes the suggestion of non-verbal communication. One day I called Luke out to the hallway and told him we were going to do something fun. I put my finger on my cheek and I explained that this was going to be a special signal just between us. Every time he looked up and saw me with my finger on my cheek, he needed to stop tapping his fingers. It worked so well that he wound up eventually stopping his habit altogether.

Mrs. B. came in for a conference, and we had a lengthy conversation about Luke's birth. She was a chemist and continued to work while he was in utero. Her theory was that something she ingested unwillingly affected his brain during his development. We thought it might have been lead poisoning. She had an extremely high IQ and believed in the holistic approach to Luke's problems; she would not let Luke take Ritalin, which was the drug of choice by doctors to treat ADHD at that time. Mrs. B. did her research and found a new treatment instead. She took Luke to the Princeton Biofeedback Center where they put him on a special formula that he was to drink three times a day. Whatever was in that formula worked. The hyperactivity ceased but it left Luke with really bad gas. We needed to open the windows by 10 a.m. She also put him on a specialized diet called the Feingold Diet, which removed all red dye #2. The theory was the elimination of that dye also eliminated hyperactivity. Perhaps the formula in combination with the diet worked even better.

A funny thing did happen that year. On our end of the year visit to the Philadelphia Zoo we were returning to school, and I noticed Luke was stretched out in the back seat of the bus sound asleep. The bus driver had slipped him a mickey. She unknowingly gave him a Tastykake junior to eat with his lunch. The chocolate had a reverse effect oh him. Instead of making him more stimulated from the caffeine, he became more calm and sleepy. There was a theory at that time to give a cup of coffee to an ADHD student if a parent was against drugs. It had the same effect as the chocolate.

Sharon Benaderet-Cohen

At our most important conference in November, Mrs. B. told us a most important fact about Luke. He never learned how to play music by reading notes, yet he could listen to a piece by Bach or Beethoven one time and play it back. Bingo! Luke was a savant and gifted in this area. I immediately went to the music teacher and informed him of Luke's special talent. He decided to put Luke in the Holiday show and the Spring Concert. He would play his pieces of Bach and Beethoven during intermission. Luke was a tremendous success. Not only did he play well, but he earned the respect of his peers and all of the families in the audience. In the spring I recommended him for the gifted music program. Imagine that. A special ed student in the gifted and talented program.

A lightbulb went off in my head! I had discovered the "good" in this student and I immediately tapped into that "good." If Luke was an auditory learner, we could tap into his strength and use it to his advantage. I arranged a meeting between his mom and a third grade teacher. Until now Luke had remained in my self-contained class since kindergarten. "Mainstreaming" was the trend in those days. We decided to mainstream him for social studies for one period a day. The class was learning all of the states and their capitals. Luke's Mom volunteered to record them using a tape recorder and a cassette. Luke listened to the tape each night while falling asleep. He got hundreds on all of his tests, and he knew the capitals inside and out. One of the proudest moments of my career was when the third grade teacher came to see me. She said all of her students wanted to do what Luke was doing because they wanted to get hundreds, too. How about that, "special ed" was teaching regular education how they could learn better!

With all of the vast accomplishments this young man made in my classroom, the icing on the cake was our class play. Every spring a class volunteered to put on a play. Why not? I never considered my class special ed. I just knew each student was special in his or her own way. It was time to make our class shine. Hedy and I wrote an Arbor Day Play with "Peanuts" characters. We made Luke act the character of Linus. Each of my communications handicapped students became stars that day. Just because they were labeled such didn't mean you had to believe it. They just had some language delays and needed to learn differently. We said a big prayer behind the curtain, and each one came shining through.

One thing you should never do as a teacher or parent is teach to a label. You need to teach to that child. I looked out at the audience, and there wasn't a dry eye among my staff, nor the parents in the audience. My principal was smiling from ear to ear. She hugged me and said, "My dear, that's why I hired you. You have the talent to inspire children!" I saved the video of that play, which was a special memory that I will never forget. Whenever I had a bad day, I would look back on that day when my class shone like the stars!

Several years ago I received a Christmas card from Luke's mother. She told me that he had graduated high school and had gotten an Associate of Science Degree in music and was writing his own music. He had a job in a local supermarket, lived on his own, and drove a car. "Oh, and by the way, Mrs. Cohen," she wrote, "he has Asperger's, which is an offshoot of Autism, but higher functioning."

He sent me a beautiful letter and a picture of himself. He is presently 39 years old and has become a success. Luke's letter thanked me and told me he remembered everything we had done in my class. He even remembered our class trips to a restaurant in Chinatown and the Mexican Food Factory (which tied into my units of study in school). My culminating activity was taking them to a restaurant. They thought they were having fun, but I was teaching them to be little people. They were kind and well-mannered to the waiters. They even behaved appropriately when marching around Chinatown. I guess I was considered a renegade teacher in those days, but I believed in teaching the "whole" child.

Excerpts from her letter include: "You have treated Luke calmly and lovingly. Over the years he's needed much extra concern, and your support has always been there. Your constant positive attitude toward Luke has helped him develop a good self-image. For all this and so much more we thank you very, very much. If all teachers cared about their pupils as much as you have about Luke, we'd have fewer problems in the world and more well-adjusted adults. Thanks ever so much!!"

The letters from Luke and his mother remain in a special notebook I purchased when I began teaching. Whenever I received a letter from a parent, an administrator, a co-worker or a student, I saved all of them in this notebook. Then whenever I had a bad day and felt like a failure, I pulled out my special notebook and read all of the cards and letters. I advise my student teachers to do the same. It's a heck of a positive strategy that they don't teach you in college!!

Notes

Chapter 2
Dignity

When you think of the word dignity, you conjure up the words "self-esteem" and "self-worth." The lengths the parents in these two stories went to help their children match those words. They loved their sons with their hearts and souls and gave them dignity until the very end.

Charlie

We had just completed our evaluation on Charlie, which contained academics, a psychological, and a social testing. All of the scores indicated that he was not learning disabled, yet there seemed to be something wrong neurologically. Charlie had been having difficulties with his balance as well as a decline in his fine and gross motor skills. We were shocked when the neurological results came back from C.H.O.P. (Children's Hospital of Philadelphia). Charlie was diagnosed with an inoperable brain tumor and had six months to live. Our team decided on home instruction since he was fine academically. A volunteer teacher went to his house for two hours a day for instruction. Charlie was in first grade and was only six years old.

To our surprise, the doctors were wrong, and Charlie made it through first grade with the teaching plan in place. What happened at the beginning of second grade was a shock I will never forget. The voice at the other end of the phone was Charlie's mom. Since Charlie was outliving his diagnosis, she requested he be placed in a regular second grade class with medical assistance. Since he was not in special education, we had to honor her request. She wanted her son to experience normalcy before he passed away. In other words, she wanted him to die with "dignity."

My director immediately developed a plan. The elementary school he was to attend was small with only one classroom per grade. The second grade teacher who was going to have him was on the verge of a nervous breakdown. Our plan was proactive. My director developed an in-service assembly in order to educate the entire staff, including teachers, classroom assistants, secretaries, and custodians as well as visiting nurses, about Charlie's condition and needs.

We were all ready for Charlie on the first day of school when he arrived by para transit on a prone board with a tracheotomy tube in his throat and breathing apparatus under the table. All he could do was blink his eyes. When his teacher instructed him for reading, he blinked with a response. The visiting nurse stayed very close to him. On Halloween his mother paraded his table and all of the apparatus. You see, she wanted him to have memories of school before he died. She wanted her son to die with dignity at all cost. That December, Charlie passed away right before Christmas. The funeral service was packed with staff. In retrospect, our school provided a safe environment for him at his mother's request. We found her "good" and worked with her son to the best of his "good." His mom got what she wanted. She gave her son normalcy to take with him to heaven. I hope we all learned a positive message through this belief, and I hope on the day he died he did have his dignity.

Kerry

It was a Monday morning and our superintendent called a meeting with our Child Study Team. I had a deep suspicion that this was going to be something big. Every seat in his large conference room was taken. Kerry's parents sat quickly as we went around the table introducing ourselves. There were doctors and specialists from St. Christopher's Hospital in Philadelphia. They explained that Kerry had Neuroblastoma, or brain cancer. He was five years old and had never experienced school since he had lived in a hospital since his diagnosis. Due to his condition he needed to be in isolation most of the time due to the germs. His parents had requested that he attend school so he could know what it is like before he passed away. We agreed to evaluate him academically and cognitively in order to place him correctly.

My partner John and I entered Kerry's residence and were given instructions by his mother. Kerry had a permanent oxygen tube in his nose and a feeding tube in his stomach. Under no circumstances were we to go near those areas. John began testing this beautiful blonde-haired little boy. He worked quickly as he chunked the testing into smaller sizes. I tested Kerry very quickly, also giving him frequent breaks. Mom informed us of Kerry's tremendous energy. He also loved singing along with his own special recording of the "Kerry" song that was made for him at the hospital. That afternoon will never be forgotten. Kerry knew the names of all of the dinosaurs, and we watched him light up. He danced around with us to his special tune. He was just a cutie patootie.

In between sessions this little boy amazed us. He was able to identify all of the letters of the alphabet, numbers one to ten, in addition to the sounds of the letters of the alphabet. He passed all cognitive tests. I kept looking at his mother and tried to identify with her. She knew her son was going to die, yet she seemed so strong.

Our tests indicated that he was not in need of a special education placement. He was a five-year-old little boy with average cognitive ability and strong academics. Our big dilemma came when we needed to place him. The two kindergarten classes had 25 students each. Our big concern was the active movements of the children, and of course the germs. We had a very small preschool class for four-year-olds that seemed perfect.

We invited the teacher to join us at our meeting to review his special needs. She was very open to the idea and welcomed Kerry to her class. This teacher went to the highest degree calling a meeting with her students to prepare them. Kerry was permitted to participate in most activities, and the class took precautions about the germs. She realized he had a very short attention span, so she gave him the job of office messenger. My office door remained open quite often. I can remember Kerry's smile as he walked around the halls. This teacher tapped into his "good" and went with his need for movement. He already had the academic skills her class offered. Many of the staff remembered this little boy's smile.

Kerry passed away on the last day of school. It was as though his spirit hung in there until it was time. I had never seen a casket that small. So tiny, and it contained such a special life. Dinosaurs decorated the walls everywhere. His mom hugged us and thanked us for making Kerry's last month special. He laughed and learned but most of all he was "normal." He had made friends. Again, a mother's instinct found the "good" in her own son. We gave her her

Sharon Benaderet-Cohen

last wishes for him. Our faculty never forgot that little bundle of happiness and his contagious smile.

Notes

Chapter 3
Trust

Building positive relationships is the most important thing you need to do. Not only do you need to do this with your students, but with their parents as well. In today's world many students are being raised by their grandparents and other extended family members. Trust is something they earn from you when you are truly there for their child. They can sense your sincerity, compassion, and confidence and, in turn, return it to you.

Big Momma

It was my second summer as a Learning Disabilities Teacher/ Consultant in my new school district. This district was blue collar with a dedicated group of parents. This was a school population with which I loved to deal. The parents seemed to be very concerned about their children's welfare and education. One Friday afternoon my superintendent came to me and said, "Cohen, we want to put you on a case. We know you have a gift working with very difficult parents, and we want you to work with a very hesitant parent. She is raising her grandson who is presently in kindergarten and he needs to be evaluated by the child study team."

I had her meet me in my office to review her grandson's needs. She was a very large African-American woman who weighed about 350 pounds. She referred to herself as "Big Momma;" so did her grandson. She was a bus driver for another school district in New Jersey and was doing her best in trying to raise her grandson. Dominic's father lived in Trenton and he was the biggest drug dealer on the East Coast. His father had received special education and she was very unimpressed about how he turned out, and she would not give her permission to have him evaluated. We knew that a parent/guardian had 51% of the vote, and our hands were tied to get this little boy the help that he needed.

She left that Monday on a very negative note. I reported her conversation to my director and told her I wasn't giving up. I called Big Momma every Friday night as a scheduled conversation to develop a special relationship with this woman. We discussed how things were different in special education when her son was in school. We could really help her grandson before entering first grade if she would just give us a chance. Speaking with Big Momma weekly was going the extra mile, but it paid off. Developing growing confidence in me, as I was in her, helped me create a positive relationship in our abilities. My superintendent really appreciated what I had done, but I looked at it like it was money in the bank. My time spent with her was well spent because it allowed us to help Dominic.

Although, Dominic's academics improved, he was still displaying some behavioral difficulties. While he was outside playing at recess, his hand went up a little girl's skirt. Administration handled it by hiring more aides on the playground.

Touch a Life

They had specific orders to keep Dominic and the little girl at opposite ends of the playground. Big Momma developed a strong dislike for the principal she needed to meet with periodically. We would all sit around a very large conference table with Big Momma at the head. She would face the wall and not even acknowledge the principal's existence. I needed to be the intermediary, which was what my job description was. I was trained to be the middle between the parent and the Administrator. Our principal was very matter of fact with the parents, whereas my training was to get them to be on my side. We needed to work together to do the best for their child. Having a very calm, caring demeanor helps me care just as much as they do. Together, we would work on a plan to help their child in the best manner possible. This belief is something I instill in my student teachers. At the beginning of each school year, make a positive phone call home for each child. Then when you need to call with something negative, they will back you. At every Child Study Team meeting I greet each parent with kindness and concern for their child, and we always shake hands firmly and positively.

Big Momma not only signed on the dotted line for her grandson to be evaluated, but we continued to have a very special relationship for Dominic's six years of elementary school. I acted as intermediary between her and certain administrators. She knew she could call me with any concerns. I had developed the confidence she had in me because she knew I genuinely cared about her grandson. One day while Dominic was in sixth grade, Big Momma came to my office very upset. She told me her blood pressure was too high; she had tears in her eyes. She was forced to give up custody to her son. Dominic was going back to live with his father in Trenton.

That meeting with Big Momma was probably the toughest meeting I had ever had. I worked so hard that summer developing a very special relationship with a very special woman. I had built a relationship based on trust, confidence, and compassion. Now, sadly, it was ending. Today I focus on the "good" we found in Dominic, and we developed a program to find that "good." Always remember, the most important thing that two people can do is to develop and build a positive relationship. Trust is earned, not given. Big Momma gave me a big hug with tears in her eyes as she left the room. She will always have a special place in my heart!

Willie

My director called me into her office to discuss a very difficult predicament. Willie's father had just registered him to attend our elementary school. He had just brought his family from Brazil. His wife spoke fluent Portuguese and no English. While in Brazil she had not sent him for any formal education. Willie had missed the first four years of his education. We met with his parents due to this dilemma. When an ELL (English Language Learner) student moves into a school district, they may not be evaluated by a Child Study Team initially to determine if there were any signs of a learning disability. Willie was just considered to be ELL. However, his lack of a formal education was certainly going to impact his educational performance. We were a very small district, and my director could be very creative in developing a program for Willie. She pulled our best ESL teacher in and told her that she was going to work one-on-one with him all morning. In period one she was to teach him reading, in period two language, and period three, math. Each period was going to last one hour. After lunch he could remain with his regular third grade class for specials (art, gym, music, and library) as well as social studies and science.

His program was designed especially to meet his needs. Hopefully, in these classes he would be exposed to the English language. I pulled from a collection of first grade materials for his teacher to use.

    Mr. G., Willie's dad, was a pilot at McGuire Air Force Base. He gave me his phone number with instructions to call him at any time. I could not call Mrs. G. due to the language barrier. The only problem occurred when he was deployed. He told me that he trusted me implicitly to make any major decision changes regarding his son. Together we had built a positive relationship and a level of trust. Willie made excellent progress with this program until the end of his elementary school years. Now it was time for him to move to our middle school.

    All of the accommodations we made for Willie were outstanding in third and fourth grades. However, middle school proved more of a challenge. I brought a second grade Everyday Math kit to Willie's new math teachers; they left it in my office. They looked at me and said they would not need it. Our school district worked with the Inclusion model and they wanted me to trust them. Mike and Pete were the middle school's pride of what inclusion should look like. Pete explained that Willie would receive the same broad overview of the topic. Then Mike would call several students to his back table to chunk it into smaller parts and reteach the lesson in a different way. I trusted Mike and Pete because they were the exemplary inclusion teachers. When one walked into the room, you couldn't tell which one was the regular education teacher and which one was the special education teacher. They team taught so well that they were seamlessly meshed. Willie was in great hands. He had Mike and Pete for Math and Science, and I knew they were going to find his "good" and teach to it. Hopefully, his team of teachers for reading and language would understand Willie's unique needs.

    Willie continued in our middle school for the next three years. His dad continued to be deployed from McGuire, trusting me with his son's educational program. Willie's mom continued to speak only Portuguese for the duration of those years. A funny meeting happened towards the end of eighth grade. We had his mom and dad come in for a meeting to meet with our teachers.

Willie was the most outstanding student in our ESL program. His dad and mom entered the room and sat down. We now knew why his dad married his mom. She was a beautiful blonde with very large bosoms. In a seated position her thong was sticking out of her pants. It was a kind of humorous way to end the year. Dad had expressed to us how he was so pleased with his son's progress. He told me that he trusted us to do the best for his son, and we did. Willie had caught up to his appropriate grade level and was graduating eighth grade as the valedictorian of his class. His parents trusted us, we trusted our teachers, and Willie flourished.

Building positive relationships begins with developing a level of trust with your students. Parents need to build positive relationships with their child's teachers, but most of all our plan worked so well because we trusted our teachers to do their best for our student. We as a district found the "good" in Willie, and we all taught to it. Tears of joy once again flowed down our faces when Willie gave his Valedictorian speech!

Notes

Chapter 4
Kindness

Dealing with students with severe disabilities can definitely be challenging. They cannot overcome their disability; however, you can help their families to get their "good" and work toward maintaining it. It is imperative that you build positive relationships with not only them, but their parents, and any other parts of their medical team.

Eddie

Eddie joined our school towards the end of second grade. He was placed in a regular class since his academics and behavioral considerations were all normal. We began noticing he would fall occasionally for no reason at all. His falls became more often towards the end of the school year. On the first day of third grade I saw Jean, his mother, wheeling him in a wheelchair. I asked if I could talk to her. She had tears in her eyes as she told me he had been diagnosed with Duchenne's Muscular Dystrophy over the summer. She educated me on the types of Muscular Dystrophy, and Duchenne's was the worst type. Her eyes filled with tears. She explained that a child with this type wasn't expected to live beyond 18 years of age. We did a lot of crying that day. How could a little boy be normal and then a few months later be diagnosed with the rarest type of a deadly disease?

Eddie's third grade teacher had a student in her class with very special needs. And he had a mother who would go to the ends of the earth for her young son. Eddie managed to get all A's in his academics. Socially, he had established many friendships. However, his muscles weakened and became more atrophied.

The most challenging time for Eddie was toileting. He simply could not move his body from the wheelchair to the toilet without help. We had a team meeting to brainstorm ideas with Jean. Our solution was to hire a one-to-one aide for Eddie. My superintendent creatively came up with a unique idea. We had a custodian named Big Jim who was over six feet tall and quite strong. What if we hired Jim to be Eddie's one-on-one aide. Eddie was quite pleased with the suggestion as was Jim. They already had a mutual admiration for each other. Jim assisted in the classroom for the minor tasks Eddie needed to do.

The challenge came when it came to toileting. Jim would pull Eddie's sweatpants down to lift him onto the toilet and then lift him back to his wheelchair. When this began to bother Jim's back, he came up with a unique solution. He would have Eddie grab onto Big Jim's thumb to lift him onto the toilet. Then one day Big Jim's thumb broke. Eddie had continually gained weight, and it took its toll on Big Jim's thumb.

We needed a new plan. I did some research on equipment that could help us. I discovered a lift at a school for students with significant disabilities. Jean, Big Jim, and I all met at this school with the occupational therapist. She put Eddie on the lift and lifted him on to the toilet. Problem solved, so we thought. It was going to cost our school district $3,000 a month to rent this lift from this facility.

Back to the drawing board. We realized that it would be more effective and a better place for Eddie to place him at this facility, rather than bring the lift to us. This facility had a class for students with normal cognitive abilities. Eddie appeared okay with the change. Our elementary school only went up to fourth grade, so he was making the change one year sooner.

In the meantime, Jean called me with a strange request. She explained that her son cried each night because he hated wearing jogging suits. They made him feel self-conscious as he did not look like his peers. I listened to her and felt her pain. It led me to meet with the Occupational Therapist again. She had a brilliant solution. Opening a catalog, she showed me pictures of clothing that looked like normal shirts and jeans. We ordered them immediately. These jeans looked like they had zippers, and the shirts also looked "normal." Jean went out and bought Eddie regular sneakers with ties instead of those with Velcro. I will always remember Eddie's smile when he arrived in one of those outfits. He had a smile from ear to ear. He looked like he won a million dollars. We had not found the "good" in the student, we found the "good" in his mother. We helped her normalize her son.

Every time I visited Eddie's new school to evaluate another student I made it my business to stop in his room to say hi. Each time Eddie's motor skills progressed to get much worse. Initially, he could give me a high five. Several years later, he could just about raise his hand. He was no longer able to write. His right hand hardly raised off the table. I lost touch with Jean when she married her boyfriend, but I have a strong feeling Eddie is no longer with us. I will never forget his beautiful smile!

Touch a Life

Louise

Louise was a second grader in a small, selfcontained classroom. She had Spina Bifida and was in a wheelchair. Spina Bifida is a birth defect in which there is incomplete closing of the backbone. Louise was born with the inability to walk due to paralysis in the lower extremities. She also had cognitive delays and a loss of bladder control. Having a student with this disability doesn't impede their ability to learn; however, there may be other problems that occur.

One day I was visiting Louise's classroom, and her teacher invited me in to observe something. She asked me if I smelled something. There was a very strong odor of urine. Louise needed to wear diapers, and many days they were more full than others. I called her mom to see if she could deliver some extra diapers to leave in the nurse's office. Louise's mom was very limited in her ability to move quickly. She was a single mom raising a handicapped child with no family support system.

Since it took a couple of weeks to get the extra diapers, I listened to our school nurse constantly complaining. By the time Louise came down to get changed, Louise's back was drenched in urine. Finally, I asked my director if I could take matters into my own hands as her case manager. I went to BJ's and bought a large supply of diapers. The problem got worse instead of getting better. Our nurse came up with an idea that needed to be discussed with Louise's urologist.

We had a phone conference with him while Louise's mom sat with us. The idea was to catheterize Louise so she wouldn't be drenched in her own urine. This was not only affecting her teacher and classmates, but it was having an effect on Louise's self-esteem. She was losing friends.

The doctor put it in writing that she could have a catheter in her to prevent the diaper flooding. Each day after lunch Louise was to wheel herself to the school nurse to get catheterized.

The plan worked well until we developed a new problem while she was in fourth grade. Louise had become larger, and it was more difficult for her mom to get her in and out of the wheelchair. We began noticing the smell returning. In conversations with her mom we asked about Louise's bathing habits. Mom admitted she had to bathe Louise less frequently because she was like lifting dead weight. It had become much more difficult to maneuver her into the tub.

John and I brainstormed ways we could help. We stopped at their apartment to take a look at the situation. We visually assessed a situation that would work. We came back and told our director that two pieces of equipment could help her mom tremendously. They were a bench that could be placed in the bathtub and a handheld showerhead. She gave us permission to purchase them but then we needed to install them. John wanted to go over himself; however, he was not permitted due to liability. He was employed by the school district as a school psychologist, not as a handyman. I called the apartment; they asked me to deliver the items and they would have the super install them.

What a difference this made in this little girl's life. Once mom got her on the bench, she could bathe with her mom's minimal assistance. We all had helped Louise find her "good." The next hurdle Louise needed to get over was transportation to and from school. Her mom drove her each way, and Louise's weight had become an issue. Our middle school had a phenomenal PTO or Parent Teacher Organization. We decided to do fundraising to get a lift van for her mom since she couldn't afford one on her own. Our schools always did dress down Fridays, where the teachers and staff could pay $5.00 to wear jeans. It took a year and a half of fundraising, but with all the money we raised, we were able to purchase a beautiful new van that had a wheelchair lift. I remember her mom's face beaming with pride when she drove up in it the first time with her daughter. With our school's generosity, we helped Louise's mom find the "good!" This "good" came in the form of helping a family so much, and it doesn't get better than that!

Notes

Chapter 5
Positivity

A positive attitude should always be maintained. The following three stories exemplify that word, each in their own way. Even though we had our ups and downs with each story, a positive attitude shone through with these students and their parents.

Barbara

Our team had just completed our evaluations on Barbara, and it was time to meet with her parents. After extensive testing we came to the conclusion that she needed to be retained in kindergarten.

Her skills showed developmental gaps, and in our best judgement retention was be in her best interest. Her parents wanted some time to think about it so they left without signing. One week went by and the two of them stormed into our office and demanded our protocols, which were our test booklets. I had learned in graduate school that this booklet was my possession, not the parents'. To my surprise my director informed me that it was indeed

Touch a Life

their possession. They wanted their attorney to review all test booklets. They took them and left. Lo and behold on the first day of school, Barbara's name appeared on the first grade list. We said our prayers and held our breath.

In November right after conferences, Barbara's teacher called me in to review Barbara's work samples. She was extremely concerned that her students were on double digit addition and Barbara still could not identify the number seven. I informed her about our experiences with the family and their refusal to retain Barbara. Now she was into the first quarter of first grade with very low skills. My director gave us permission to evaluate her based on first grade, but we needed a parent's signature. In a phone conversation with Barbara's mom, she told me that she had full custody of Barbara, and that she and her dad were not married. She was now in agreement for the testing but could not leave her job. I remember driving to her bank and having her sign the paperwork over the counter. She was now on board to do whatever she could to see her daughter succeed.

Our testing was completed within one week and we found her to have learning disabilities. With her mom's permission we were able to place her in a self-contained small class for students with multiple disabilities. Barbara learned at a very slow but steady pace. More difficulties were noted regarding her parents. They did not see eye-to-eye, nor did they share custody. We needed to have all documents and letters sent to separate addresses. Also, we went the extra mile and accommodated each parent by having separate meetings. All seemed fine until Barbara was scheduled to leave our elementary school and go to fifth grade. During one of our meetings, I had the surprise of my life. After meeting with her mom and getting a signature to attend our middle school with special education help, I met with her dad in a small room near the office. This was as usual, and I did not see this coming. This tall African-American man stood towering over me screaming that he wanted to get his daughter the f**k out of special education and that I should place her in all regular education classes next year. He wanted the label removed. His voice got louder and it was dismissal time.

Thank goodness my co-worker heard the screaming and opened the door. He acknowledged how upset and agitated he got and asked him to calm down and come back another day. Barbara's dad followed my co-worker, who happened to be a school psychologist, to debrief in the principal's office. He did so and came back calmer and signed for Barbara to continue to receive the special education help she needed. That was the last day I ever scheduled a meeting alone with a possibly explosive parent. I recommend to every teacher that if you feel you are going to have a conference with an angry parent, have a co-worker join you in that meeting. Do not go in alone!

Barbara's programming for special education became less and less while in middle school. I continued meeting with each parent separately, and they became more and more supportive. When leaving our middle school, Barbara was scheduled to be in all regular education classes. At eighth grade graduation, her dad was nowhere in sight. Her mom was there with balloons and flowers for her beautiful daughter. She kissed me on the cheek and thanked me for being Barbara's case manager for the past eight years. Barbara hugged me and thanked me as well. What I have to take away from this story is that a mother's instinct kicked in, and she finally wanted the best for her child. She helped us to find the "good" in Barbara's as well and teach to that "good." Over eight years Barbara was instructed with a curriculum that matched her specific needs. I often wonder what would have happened if we had done as her father wanted. In this case mom knew best. I will never forget Barbara's shining smile on her graduation day. You can't put a price on that!

Kriss

Kriss began in our PreSchool. His classroom was at the end of the hallway. He would have tantrums so bad that his screams could be heard throughout the hallways. One day Kriss began escaping and attempted to run down the hall. My superintendent was a thin man who stood about 6'6" tall. My most vivid memory was when they announced an escape in the preschool program. He dashed to pick Kriss up, placed him under his arm, and returned Kriss safely to his room. All the while, Kriss was kicking and screaming. This is how we spent most of the summer school program. By kindergarten, his mom and dad knew Kriss had a problem. His mom was an educator; she worked as a principal in a high school in North Jersey.

We quickly evaluated Kriss, classified him Emotionally Disturbed, and placed him in a small special education class. Kriss remained in these types of classes that emphasized behavior throughout elementary school.

In the beginning of fifth grade we had a problem. Kriss had become quite depressed, and John, our school psychologist, was trying to get to the bottom of this. Throughout his conversation with Kriss there was a common thread. He was tired of being in all special education classes and wanted to fly. As a learning specialist I knew Kriss was functioning at a second grade level in reading, language, and math. My gut level intuition said Kriss should remain in a self-contained program. John had the opposite opinion. He felt that Kriss needed to have an opportunity to be in a regular education class. This was the only time in 13 years together that John and I disagreed. John convinced me that Kriss's self-esteem would suffer if we didn't at least try. At the beginning of the second marking period we placed

Kriss in regular classes for reading and social studies. Our fifth grade classes were divided into teams where one teacher taught two subjects. We had many meetings to prepare her for Kriss. He hadn't had a tantrum in many years. On day one we all held our breath. When his teacher handed out a worksheet on a fifth grade level, she differentiated instruction to meet his needs. This worked very well for the remainder of the year.

By the end of fifth grade Kriss had made such excellent progress we programmed him to participate in full regular ed classes in all subjects. Kriss began smiling and no longer seemed depressed. He beamed with his mother at the eighth grade graduation. I asked him if he remembered me since I had retired the prior year. He hugged me and said, "Of course I do." He had a smile from ear to ear. Kriss had tremendous pride. He had advocated for himself and found his own "good." He fought for something he believed in, and earned it, and we found a teacher who taught to that "good." This was the first child we had in 13 years of working with each other who took matters into his own hands and developed his own "good."

Carl

After 11 years of working in New Jersey, I moved across the bridge to Pennsylvania as a special education teacher. What I discovered was that the grass is not always greener on the other side of the bridge. I had gotten a $7,000 raise because I was hired by what was known as the best district in Bucks County. After an intense interview process, the director informed me that I scored a 4.0 in the interview with 1250 applicants applying for the job. My class consisted of 12 learning disabled students in grades 4, 5, and 6. I was used to cooperative parents in my former district, but these were unbelievable. One father had some concerns about his son and asked me to meet with me at 7:30 a.m. I explained to him that school didn't begin until 8:30. His reply was that he was a very important lawyer who had 25 staff working under him so he needed to meet at 7:30. My principal gave me instructions to do so.

Another example was my individual behavior plan for one student. He was working on completing a behavior chart for work and behavior points for the week. He and his mother decided on a sleepover with his friend as a reward. The student did not obtain his goal so I informed his mom to not give him his reward. On Monday morning he came into my room, walked over to the kidney-shaped table where I taught reading, and put his feet up onto my desk. On his feet were a pair of sneakers that cost $125. He boasted that he didn't need my sleepover, because his mom bought him these fantastic sneakers. It wasn't how much they cost that bothered me, it was his attitude. This attitude was generally the same for all of the students in my class. They seemed entitled. Many of them had maids, au pairs, and lived in very expensive homes. Their attitudes displayed that they thought they were better than everyone else.

It was the week before Christmas vacation, which was to begin on Friday afternoon. I had totaled up my students' points for classwork and behavior. Carl had not earned all of his points for the week. Our reward that they had worked on was to earn their lunchtime holiday party. Carl kept asking me if he still could participate in the party. One rule I always believed in was, "Say what you mean, and mean what you say." If the students don't get consistency, they will never believe you. I could not go back on my word. I asked Carl to bring in a brown bagged lunch for Friday afternoon. Our desks were arranged in a U, and I asked Carl to sit in the back. The pizzas were delivered on time, and my class consumed them with eagerness. I purchased a cake in the shape of a Santa Claus, and we all ate with great enthusiasm. Carl sadly ate his lunch while watching all of us eat and participate in our party. This may seem cruel, but if I went back on my word, Carl would have never believed me again.

      The first day of January arrived, and I greeted all of my students as they entered the room. At lunchtime I got a phone call and was asked to report to the main office. I nervously walked down the hallway to the office, thinking I was going to get fired. The person on the other end of the phone was Carl's mother. She thanked me for having Carl watch us eat lunch on the last day of school and missing the party. He did a lot of reflection over the vacation and was determined to never let that happen again. Carl was going to make every effort to complete all seatwork each week. She felt he turned over a new leaf and was going to follow all of my directions. She thanked me for a job well done. Carl was the perfect student in work completion and behavior for the rest of the year. By my firm expectations I had found his "good." His "good" remained intrinsic for him as he had turned into a different student with a different work ethic.

Notes

Chapter 6
Forgiveness

Some mothers are very different. They have different styles of raising their children. These two mothers did their best for their daughter and son. Sometimes they overcame challenges, and sometimes they didn't. No matter what, they tried to do their best.

Sally

It was a routine Monday morning. I was attending a meeting for Sally, who was a third grade student with type 1 or juvenile diabetes. The purpose of our meeting was to mainstream her in social studies from a self-contained special education class. Her social studies teacher needed to be apprised of Sally's medical needs. We received a total shock when her mother entered the room. This woman was strikingly beautiful, thin with a short haircut. She had a tattoo of a teardrop of blood on the front of her neck and the word DEATH tattooed on the back of her neck at the hairline. She informed us that she worked at night, leaving Sally alone. She was a stripper at the club down the street. Although her appearance was unusual, she turned out to be a tremendous advocate for her daughter.

She gave us a lesson on juvenile diabetes. Sally needed to go to the nurse each day to get one shot of insulin before lunch. She also needed to have her sugar tested by the school nurse prior to receiving the insulin. An absolute must was having a piece of fruit and cheese crackers in her desk at all times in case her sugar level dropped. She also needed a bottle of water on her desk at all times. Also, she needed to use the girl's room more frequently. Her teacher needed to let her go. The signs of diabetes include frequent drinking and peeing. She explained that Sally's blood levels spiked quite high. It could go all the way up to 800, in which case we were to call 911. Normal was 120. If her level spiked too high, it would send her into a diabetic coma.

Everything went well for a while until one day when I was in the building meeting with another teacher. I walked by Sally's social studies class and saw no water bottle on her desk. I asked her teacher where it was, and she replied she decided it wasn't fair to the other children so she took it away. If Sally had one, then all of the other students should have one, too. I asked if I could meet with her after school. When meeting with her I called upon federal law and told her that she was infringing upon Sally's civil rights. She was protected because of that law. That really struck home, and the teacher made sure her water bottle was on her desk the rest of the year. Fortunately, we never had Sally go into a diabetic coma.

Sally's mom turned out to be her biggest advocate. If Sally forgot her special snack, she would bring it immediately at any time. She only worked nights so she was available all day. We couldn't worry about Sally being alone each night. She had some help where that was concerned. You should never judge a book by its cover.

From our initial meeting we all could have judged her as a bad mother because of her strange appearance. This mother found the "good "in her medically ill daughter. Instead of complaining about all of the needs of her daughter, she championed for her. In all of my years as an educator, I have never had a more cooperative woman who genuinely cared for her child. Who was I or anyone to say what she did for a living was terrible? She provided for her child in the best way she could. No one could take that away from her.

    The person who needed forgiveness was Sally's teacher. In what she thought was fair by not providing the bottle for Sally could have brought a lawsuit, or much worse, the death of a child. It's funny how things turn for the better. In present day classrooms every child had their own water bottle. Equality for all children. Sally's story happened in the early 90s. But still, I often wonder why this teacher's solution couldn't have been similar having all of her students having a water bottle on their desks. I have worked with many diabetic students since Sally and have found many more cooperative teachers. Unfortunately, this disease has been on the rise due to an increase in childhood obesity. If you are the teacher of a student with juvenile diabetes, pay very close attention to their needs. You don't make the rules regarding their needs. Instead, you are the one who guards their medical needs. Sally's teacher needed forgiveness because in her mind this was not the "fair" thing to do.

David

    It was my first day of my new job as a learning consultant. I was assigned to test my first student who attended second grade whose teacher described him as "beyond ADHD." My school psychologist partner and I decided to team up together and test the child in the school nurse's office due to its small space. Wow! Was that a good decision. This little guy was literally climbing up and down the bookcases while we each took turns testing him. Not only was the decision a good one, but we completed our task in several hours. David was determined to be not only ADHD, but significantly learning disabled in the areas of math, writing, and reading. This was the early 90s so we concluded by placing him in a self-contained class for learning disabled students.

David did very well academically in this placement all the way through elementary school. His teachers did their best to develop strategies for his ADHD. They allowed for extra movement by giving him extra errands to go to the office along with preferential seating in the classroom. Academically, he made slow but steady progress. Our social worker, after meeting with his mother, discovered that she was a prostitute who brought her Johns over to their home while David was there. She sometimes came to parent conferences, but for the most part she was negligent.

When David was in sixth grade, I received a very important phone call asking me to meet with my director and our superintendent in his office. This was a highly confidential meeting due to its sexual nature. David had bitten a girl classmate on her breast and left a bite mark on her areola. Since his behavior was of a sexual nature, this meeting was strictly confidential. The girl had been affected not just physically, but emotionally as well. We put our heads together to assess the situation. My superintendent decided to have a meeting with us, David's teacher, his mother, and the lunchtime assistant who was on duty when the incident happened. He was planning to scare David by informing him that this might be a police matter.

The day came, and since I was David's case manager, I led the meeting. David sat at the head of this very large, intimidating conference table facing all of these adults and the girl he injured. I introduced all of the people in attendance. David just stared at everyone. I discussed the purpose for our meeting and asked David if he knew why we were meeting. My superintendent interjected and said this was very serious and could be a police matter. His voice was the most stern I had ever heard. David's mother asked if she could make a statement. What she said made everyone's jaw drop. She said, "David done what he seen my boyfriend did. He done bit my tit." We were all shocked. How does one respond to that? My superintendent emphasized that just because the child had seen this happen to his mother did not mean it was right for him to do it to another child. If David repeated this behavior again, he would be reported to the police and he would have a police record. We thought he had learned his lesson.

David wound up getting through middle school and high school with very close supervision. His mother never showed up for any other meetings. His new case managers watched him closely. He graduated from high school with no further incidents.

To my surprise, one evening during the summer after he graduated, I was listening to the eleven o'clock news. I could not believe what I heard. A murder had occurred on the route I took to school. A botched robbery by a local teenager attempting to rob a gas station had led to the knifing and death of the attendant.

The name of the teenager was David S. The next day I received a phone call from the school psychologist with whom I evaluated him with 10 years before, when he was a tiny second grader. She wanted to know if I heard the news. We could not believe it. The gas station owner died, and David stood trial as an adult. He was sentenced to life behind bars. This innocent eight-year-old boy turned into a very disturbed young man. Thank goodness he was the only student I case managed who went to jail.

These two students were both products of their environments. Both mothers were at poverty level, and each did the only thing she knew to raise their children. One solved her daughter's problems by becoming her best advocate. The second mother neglected her son and did the best she could under her own circumstances. One was a success; the other failed.

She failed, or did the system fail her?

Notes

Chapter 7
Empathy

Sometimes you deal with parents who don't really care. You can give them many suggestions, but they don't carry through. The best thing you can do is just keep trying. You never know when they will finally accept some help.

Nathan

Nathan joined our school while in second grade. According to his receiving records, he needed to be in a small self-contained special education class. The class he was placed in was a perfect placement to deal with his learning disabilities. As his new Case Manager, I spoke with his mother over the phone at her request. She was a single mom and could not take off from work to meet with us as a team. Her disclosure to me was that she was a single mom and Nathan was her foster child. If things went well she planned to adopt him.

Things went well in the beginning for him. He was able to

make slow but steady progress academically. At conference time his teacher and mother had a phone conference to meet his mom's circumstances. His teacher was very concerned that he was displaying symptoms of hyperactivity or ADHD. His mom reported that no signs were seen at home.

During the next marking period his symptoms got worse in school. We called his mom together and had a phone conference. She denied seeing any signs at home. She also informed us that Nathan attended a prayer service every Wednesday night with her. It lasted three hours, and he sat perfectly still during the entire service. We tried to gain her understanding that school was different; however, she didn't want to hear it. Finally, she mentioned it to her pediatrician who was also concerned about school reports. He prescribed a low dose of Ritalin, which is the drug they administer to students with symptoms of hyperactivity. His mom was going to begin to give it to him.

Our school policy included filling out a sheet for two weeks. We needed to give the doctor feedback so we kept notes on each period in case the drug needed to be adjusted in some way. We never noticed any changes for the better, and lo and behold we found out she never filled the prescription. Friends at her church convinced her that he was fine without any medication. Needless to say, we dropped the issue, and his teacher continued to use strategies in the classroom to accommodate his needs.

Nathan was promoted to third grade and his mother formerly adopted him. Things went well for the first marking period. Something out of the ordinary happened one morning. Nathan was found crying, all curled up on the floor right outside his classroom. He was clutching an iPad in his arms. His teacher called me immediately due to this bizarre behavior.

I ran to assist her. Nathan was crying uncontrollably. We

tried making sense of what had happened to him. He was sobbing that his mother had beaten him up and he called DYFS on her before leaving for school. DYFS was an agency to protect children from harmful parents. He had markings all over him as if someone had beaten him up. His mother was appalled that anyone thought she was a bad mother. An investigation took place, and what incurred was almost not to be believed. Nathan created the entire story in his head. DYFS was now investigating a parent for no reason. The child created the whole scenario. Our team had Nathan evaluated,' and the psychiatrist informed us that he had sociopathic tendencies and was considered a pathological liar. What happened next was something I had never encountered before. During a phone call with his mom, she disclosed to me that she had buyer's remorse. She wanted to give Nathan back.

By the time Nathan moved to our middle school things had calmed down. As his case manager, I informed each grade level team about his background. He was seen by our School Psychologist once a week and was receiving counseling twice a week on a regular basis. We utilized the services of the African-American institute to serve as a Big Brother since he had no male role model in his life.

I volunteered to be his mentor. We met every Tuesday morning in an empty office. I sensed the "good" in this young man. If only I could get through to him. We had already developed a positive relationship over the years, and I knew he trusted me. Over the years, through it all, I had developed some trust in this young man.

During our sessions we began with organizational skills since he was always losing his assignments. I bought a three-ring notebook and dividers. Also included was a pencil case, pencils, pens, and a protractor. Each week we added assignments from all five academic areas. All five of his teachers made arrangements with

Nathan's mom to e-mail her with missing assignments. Some would get three e-mails a day, but they never complained because we were working as a team to keep him afloat. I also noticed from reports that his behavior was the best in Science. I asked each teacher if I could observe their class when Nathan was in it. During my observations I noticed one thing. His behavior in all classes was mediocre. The day I observed Science they were dissecting sharks. His behavior was perfect. Could it be his interest in the topic? No, it was the unique behavior system that his new teacher created. It was only known to Nathan, his teacher, and no other students. She created a secret behavior system that was truly unique that contained non-verbal communication. This was something that really worked for this student.

I continued to meet with Nathan on Tuesday mornings for the duration of eighth grade. We eventually moved our conversations from organizational techniques to what his aspirations were after graduation. I had built a very strong relationship with this young man, and through it all I found his highest "good." He responded to the one-on-one undivided attention I gave him. It was only once a week, but I responded positively to our meetings. I actually looked forward to them.

On the day of the eighth grade graduation, I planned to meet Nathan at a doorway after the ceremony. I keenly scoped out the bleachers in the gym for his mom. It was with great pride that I stood there taking a picture with this good-looking young student. His mom proudly took some with us. Later, I congratulated each of his teachers for a job well done, along with the administration. We had all worked together to make it successful for this student. As a famous woman once said, "It takes a village to raise a child." Nathan went off to our high school. I spent an entire day preparing his new group of teachers and administration for tips on how to make it successful for Nathan. When I reflected on it, he came to us from foster care, was eventually adopted by a single mother, and raised by a very nurturing school. Nathan touched my heart in a special way. I sent him the photograph I took of us at graduation. Sometimes the single, most simple thing a student wants is your time. That's how you find the "good" in them.

Just give them your time.

Bob

After several evaluations, observations and meetings we decided to make this middle school student a Resource Room student. All indications were that he needed additional support for Reading, English and Math. His parents were invited to an IEP meeting in order to develop an Individual Educational Plan. I set the meeting for 2:45 which was close to dismissal time. All of his teachers were invited along with our School Psychologist, our school social worker, and Bob's parents. This was my first IEP meeting in my second district as a learning consultant and I wanted it to go really well.

Everyone gathered around the table and I introduced everyone. All of the teachers took turns giving their updates as to Bob's academic progress thus far in the year. John gave his cognitive test results, and I shared my academic results. Our school social worker presented the results of her report. We collectively recommended the Resource Room as a support placement. Since Bob was only having delays in his main subjects of reading, math, and English, our recommendations were to place him in smaller support classes for those classes, and he could remain in his social studies and science classes.

To my surprise the bell rang, and every teacher got up and left. I found out later on that the teachers in this district followed the

Touch a Life

contract to the tee, and they could leave at 3:20. Our social worker left since there were no home issues to discuss. To my horror, John was called out on an emergency. As the door shut behind him, something happened that I will never forget. Bob's mother asked me to tear up the IEP that we just drafted. She told me that they did not agree with our findings and they did not see Bob having any of the delays that were reported by testing and his teachers. I took one big gulp and tore it up. They left the room quietly with me sitting to ponder what happened.

During the entire ride home, I worried. Was I going to lose my job tomorrow? The next morning I went in to my director's office. I explained what happened at Bob's meeting. She replied, "Cohen, you did the right thing. Always remember the parents have 51% of the vote. If they don't agree with our findings, that's their prerogative." I replied, "But what about Bob and his academic success?" She reiterated again, "You need to separate yourself; if they don't want it, your hands are tied." I was so disappointed. In my mind, we had just found the "good" in this young man and developed the perfect program to meet his needs. I went back to the middle school to deliver the message to Bob's teachers. They were shocked and quite disappointed, too. Bob remained in all of his regular classes and graduated eighth grade with extremely poor grades.

The lessons I learned from this experience were first and foremost, the parent always has 51% of the vote. Second, don't ever schedule an important IEP meeting at the end of the day. Just because the teachers in my former district stayed beyond the sound of the bell and went beyond their contract does not mean your new group of teachers would react the same. I followed Bob's progress while he was in high school. He wound up quitting school in tenth grade. I never did keep in touch with him beyond that. Even today as I reflect, in my heart of hearts, if his parents had okayed the change to Resource support, Bob would have graduated from high school. Some parents have a belief that special education has a stigma. Perhaps they had a bad experience in their past school experience. We were so close to finding Bob's "good."

All endings in education can't be good ones. You just have to do your best in each situation.

Notes

Chapter 8
Love

These two students were to me considered Children of God, given the tragic lives each of them had endured. To know and have an understanding of true despair that someone as young as they were was beyond imaginable. With love and support, each of them flourished. It's amazing what some extra care will do for someone's self-esteem.

Ginny

Ginny joined our Communication Handicapped class in our sixth year as a class together. In those days, a self-contained class stayed together as a unit with very little changes. We acted as a little family. Ginny joined our class during the first marking period. This disheveled little girl would show up in tattered clothing with messed up hair. From the very beginning, I sensed she had severe psychiatric problems. After the other students followed along with morning routines, she would get down on the rug and put the side of her face on it and drag it all the way across the room. When she got up she had a rug burn on her face. This was the most bizarre behavior any of my students had ever displayed.

I asked my principal if I could read her confidential folder in her office. She had me come in and sat there while I read her file. I was totally shocked as I read her history and background. Both of her parents had died of heroin overdoses and left Ginny and her two brothers orphaned. This was also at the height of the AIDS epidemic. Ginny had to leave her home in California since she had no known relatives to care for her. Ginny's records indicated that she needed an institutional setting as her school placement. To my surprise, my CST Team placed her with me due to my calm, loving personality. I left my Principal's office wondering what I could do to help this little girl.

My instincts told me to document everything. Like clockwork, every Monday morning she scraped the side of her face on the carpet, rubbed it and attempted to burn it. She continued to come in each morning totally disheveled and need a change of clothing. My school nurse was an angel supplying Ginny with Vaseline for her face and a new change of clothing. I felt as though I was teaching Patti Duke as she portrayed Helen Keller in *The Miracle Worker.* Her disruptions were beginning to affect the rest of my students. I decided to dig a little deeper and found out more amazing things.

Ginny was living in a group home in our district with 14 other children. Another shocking fact occurred. Her two natural brothers were adopted by the same family. They did not want Ginny. Now I understood why Monday mornings were so difficult for Ginny. Her brothers were living in a loving home and she just spent a weekend fending for herself in a group home, surrounded with 14 other children. We decided to visit the home.

They were having a barbeque one afternoon after school. Several teachers joined me on our visit. We received a tour of this old large home that was converted to a group home. Ginny slept with four girls, ages 8 to 11. Five older girls were in another bedroom and five boys were in another bedroom. It seemed quite organized while we were there for the barbeque but we got the feeling that these children were left to their own devices when adult supervision left.

I continued to complain to my staff that Ginny's behavior was bizarre but to no avail. One morning while my school psychologist was visiting our class, something unexpected happened. My classroom assistant screamed "Ginny get that scissors out of your throat!" Ginny had just swallowed a scissors. Thank goodness my assistant had a good view of her as she put the blades down her throat. This was April, so no other placement was sought.

Then things took a turn for the better. I had a volunteer mother who came in once a week. She began bringing in beautiful barettes in and putting them into Ginny's hair. We brought in new outfits for her to wear. Ginny's self-esteem began to soar. Even her academic skills began to show slow, but steady progress. Our volunteer mother had found the secret to finding Ginny's "good." As her self-esteem improved so did she.

My most memorable moment that school year was this: Every year on the last day of school I had my students sit in a circle. We went around the circle and said what they learned in Mrs. Cohen's classroom. Our morning board story was still on the board. Ginny said, "Mrs. Cohen, watch this." She read the entire story correctly. Not only that but my entire class clapped for her. Until that day, Ginny had not yet mastered reading. I cried as my class clapped for her. We did act like a little family. Little by little, as her self-esteem grew, we were finding her "good" and teaching to it. Ginny left my class that day a new child. She moved to another district and was adopted by a loving couple. I have since lost touch with her, but I am sure she is doing well!

Sam

After teaching the same Communications Handicapped class for five years, my director informed me that they were recycling me and giving me the Multiple Disabilities Kindergarten class. Little did I know there would be a very psychiatrically involved student amongst my class.

Reading his records brought tears to my eyes. Sam's mother did not want a boy. She wanted a girl. Her solution was putting him in a waffle iron, burning him, and leaving him at the curb as if he were garbage. His grandparents who were in their 60s legally adopted him and were raising him. He never saw his mother again. This left me with a very behaviorally challenged young student.

This was a new class and its placement in the building didn't go exactly as planned. Instead of being placed in the kindergarten wing in a room with a bathroom, they put us in the fifth grade wing. This would've been fine except for Sam's bathroom habits. Instead of waiting for all of us to take a bathroom break and go to the boy's room with our group, Sam would run out of the room screaming pee-pee. He would pull down his pants and run with a naked tushy exposed. The fifth grade boys didn't know what to make of him. Some stared but most just ignored him.

The worst part of Sam's behavior were his tantrums. Everyday Sam would lie on the floor on his stomach, kicking his arms and legs screaming, "I want my mommy." Other teachers would walk by our room and look in our window, wondering if I was killing one of my students. I decided to try to break this habit. I would get down on the floor and kick and scream next to him. I would scream, "I want my mommy, too, Sam but I can't have her now." Sam was in a five-year-old body but with a two-and-a-half year old mind. During our free-time period I took note of Sam's love for playing with clay. It seemed to be his greatest pleasure. I seized the moment and called my custodian to see if we had any extra small round tables in the building. My luck was with me and the next morning my custodian delivered one to our room and placed it between my kidney-shaped table and the place where my assistant sat.

  I softened up some clay and rolled it into logs. Later I made a deal with him. From now on you can do 10 minutes of reading with Mrs. Cohen and then play with your clay for 10 minutes. Then you can do some math with my assistant and then play with clay again. Bingo! I finally found the "good" in Sam. He needed chunking learning times into short increments, and he responded to a tactile form of learning. He bought into the system and his tantrums decreased.

  They even became less intense. His bathroom habits even got better. Sam loved playing with the clay which pacified him and the shorter intervals allowed for some slow but steady academic growth.

  The last day of school finally arrived, and we ended my class in my usual way. We placed the chairs in a circle. Each child had to tell one thing they learned in Mrs. Cohen's class. Sam proudly patted himself on his back and said, "Mrs. Cohen, remember when I used to tantrum for 20 minutes at a time. Now I only tantrum for 2 minutes at a time." My whole class applauded, and he was beaming from ear to ear. I was so proud of him I couldn't stop smiling. Sam had found his own "good." This little guy was able to note the improvement in his behavior. Academic progress is important, but so is progress in behavior. And when a child sees it in himself, it doesn't get any better than that!

Notes

Chapter 9
Celebrate

These three stories have a common thread. Each began with a dislike of some kind. Danny invoked fear. Peter was a student who invoked dismay, and Katie was a co-worker who sparked confusion. All three had these character traits in them. However, each of their stories sparked a celebration!

Dennis

It was the last week of the school year and all of the teachers were busy packing up their classrooms. I was busy covering my bulletin boards since I was coming back to the same classroom, so I could leave my student books and teacher's manuals on the shelves and carefully cover them with newspaper. Everything was going well. My students were actively involved with their end of the year packets. My co-worker, our association president, came in and said, "Cohen, I just heard you are getting Dennis S. in your room next year." My heart sank and my fear showed on my face.

Touch a Life

My class was in its fourth year together as the commnications handicapped classroom. I did not want Dennis in my classroom; his story preceded him. He supposedly was so bad that he had caused his prior teacher a nervous breakdown. What could I do to get out of this? I asked for a conference to meet with my principal to look at his cumulative folder. This was a big mistake for what I read frightened me all the more. It said his placement was to be in a private school setting for very disturbed students. She explained to me that Dennis's mother was our school board president. She had heard of my reputation and my calm personality so she decided on placing him in my room. Damn, I was a victim of my loving personality again.

I went home and worried over the entire summer. I walked around with a knot in my stomach that would not go away. The first day of school came and I sat Dennis front and center of my room. The other desks were arranged in rows since I didn't know what behaviors to expect.

Dennis began to flap his hands under his chin almost continually. This is very typical behavior for an autistic student. He also loved to keep our classroom ball on his lap to stimulate himself. In those days squishy balls were in vogue. Over the next few months, with a lot of hard work, I used the squishy ball to keep his tactile behavior channeled and had broken his behavior of flapping. Our school psychologist informed me the ball rubbing was a form of masturbation and it should eventually become less.

Dennis became more normalized as the year went on. His reading and other academic areas improved. My squishy ball helped Dennis to find his "good." This technique broke him of his very bad habit. Most of all the demons that I expected from what was written in his cumulative folder did not pan out for me. The only bad day I had with him was when we were taking the Iowa exams. These were state tests designed to measure academic progress. Dennis put his head down on his desk over his test booklet and began to shut down. My instincts went into play. I slammed down on the desk and said in a very loud voice, "Dennis, you cannot shut down now!" Miraculously, he lifted his head and began to take the test. I often asked myself what I would've done if he had not responded that well. In February my class was planning a trip to Chinatown since we had studied the Chinese New Year. We went to eat dim sum at a restaurant and then walk around Chinatown. My co-workers thought I was crazy because of the behaviors of some students. I only brought my classroom assistant and no volunteer mothers. My experience taught me that my students behaved worse when their mothers joined us. I divided us into groups of four each.

To my surprise and very great pleasure, Dennis's behavior was outstanding. He ordered well and displayed the best manners. When we walked around Chinatown he was perfect. He didn't try to wander without us or try to leave the group. The next morning I got a phone call from his mother. She said, "Sharon, you're the only person I know who could get my son to eat octopus. And, overall, my son has done so well in your class. Lady, you are worth your weight in gold."

I thanked her and told her I, too, was very fortunate to have had the opportunity to have him in my class. When administrators came in to observe me, they didn't see anything out of the ordinary. They saw Dennis behaving appropriately just because I worked hard at the beginning I found his "good" and utilized my instruction towards meeting his needs.

Several lessons were learned that year. First of all, do not listen to any negative reports that prior teachers have made. Do not read your cumulative folders for the first three weeks of the school. Of course, read the list of medications you need to know. After three weeks, you can read them because you have been able to judge the student on their own. This child was scheduled to go to a private setting, yet his mother intervened. He was a success in my classroom even though his prior teacher had a negative experience with him. The old adage fits so well here: "Don't judge a book by its cover."

As an update, Dennis left my class and went through middle school. He attended our vocational technical institute and opened his own landscaping company. Success was something we all celebrated! Personally, I celebrated Dennis in a very special way. He taught me a very special lesson. You should never fear or worry about an incoming student just because of another teacher's judgements. You never know what kind of relationship you will develop with this student and you may be very surprised!

Peter

I was asked to evaluate a two-and-a-half-year-old boy who reminded me of a cherub with his adorable cheeks and head of thick, curly hair. He made little eye contact and was echolalic. If I said a sentence, he repeated it. His problem was mainly in the communication realm. We placed him in the preschool handicapped class where he could get language support. At his age of five we placed him in a small special education class for the support he needed.

Peter continued to make academic progress in this placement for all of his elementary years. He was eventually classified Asperger's, which is an offshoot of Autism. They usually have better language skills, have better cognitive skills, but display poor social skills.

While in sixth grade Peter began missing a lot of school. We also noticed on the days he was there he constantly repeated sentences over and over again. In order to get to the bottom of this, we invited his mother in for a conference. She began crying and apologized for his absences. She had been home ill with a very bad inflammation of Fibromyalgia. She let her son take off school to help her. While in bed, she watched the old movie channel over and over again. Now we realized where Peter was getting those sentences that he repeated over and over again. He had repeated sentences absolutely accurately from the same movies.

Bingo, we had found the "good" in Peter. He could memorize lines well. We channeled this ability and placed him in the drama club. He was such a success that we placed him in the club for the next two seasons. He diligently learned his lines and a star was born!

We channeled Peter's talent or his "good" and we had the teachers teach to that "good."

We all celebrated Peter in a very special way. His mother sobbed with pride in all of his performances. We tapped into his "good" and developed his area of strength. It had always been the auditory mode all along!

Karen

My communications handicapped class was right next door to my co-worker Karen. She was a third grade teacher with 25 students and my class was self-contained with eight students. Every day six of my students were mainstreamed for social studies in other classes. They went in pairs to other rooms for instruction. This was 1986, and in those days it was called mainstreaming; now it is called inclusion. One of my students, Janet told me, "Mrs. Cohen, Mrs. N. doesn't like us very much." I even noticed that Karen treated all special education students as though they were beneath her. Also in those days we weren't attached to any particular curriculum, so I was free to come up with my own. That year I decided to teach language through studying foreign cultures. My picks were Mexico and Japan which were two diverse cultures.

Karen happened to be Asian, but I wasn't sure what country she was from. One day to my surprise she approached me. She said, "Sharon, you are beginning to study Japan with your students. I was born in Tokyo and I would like to team teach with you. Why don't we team up together?" Together we planned to teach our unit on Japan every Friday afternoon. I thought I would take my eight students into her classroom, but she insisted on moving her 25 students into my room. Our students were really excited.

The first Friday of the initiation of our mutual unit, Karen came into the room in full garb. She was wearing the most beautiful silk kimono, socks, sandals and a fan to top it off. Our students were mesmerized. She described her entire outfit. In later weeks she taught them calligraphy, sports, foods, customs, etc., once a week. I basically teamed with her as she was the primary teacher while I followed her teachings. Each week my students looked forward to our one hour with Karen and our "travels" to Japan. We decided to do a culminating activity by taking our students to the Japanese Tea Garden in Fairmont Park in Philadelphia, PA. During the week I had my students divided into small groups. My Autistic students created a food picture dictionary and my higher ability students were divided into sports and cultures. This was my first experience in differentiated instruction.

Karen had become a ray of sunshine. This was a teacher who had a low regard for special education in the beginning of the year. By teaming up with me, she spread her wings and enjoyed every minute of sharing her culture with my class. I found the "good" in Karen as she did most of the teaching. She realized that special education students were not any different than regular education students. While she taught most of our Friday afternoon adventures,

Sharon Benaderet-Cohen

I was there to make accommodations for those who needed it. From the first day of that unit, she had a new respect for my class and she really fell in love with them. Karen's "good" came through by working directly with them. My team teaching with her found her highest good as an educator!

To this day, when I look back on this experience, I celebrate my co-worker! She offered her services to a co-worker. In today's schools we are much more diverse. Multiculturalism is a topic that I teach in my educational theory class at Penn State.

With schools that are rich in diversity, take advantage of co-workers who are from other countries. They can even come in for one day to teach your students about their culture.

I had a student teacher two years ago who was from India. She was teaching first grade and part of the curriculum was teaching holidays around the world. The best lesson she did was coming in a costume that she wore on Denali, or India's New Year's celebration. She shared a short video and then read them a story about that holiday. Her students were totally mesmerized and it was her best lesson. Celebrate other cultures and the rich diversity we now have. Invite parents of other cultures to do the same. If you are an educator from another culture, volunteer to do the same for a co-worker. In other words, celebrate!

Notes

Chapter 10
Compassion

Chronic illnesses are very difficult to deal with. Some have better outcomes than others. As a teacher you just have to deal with them and do the best you can. Expect the most productive possible.

Jamie

Jamie joined our fifth grade class in November. His mother informed us that he had Tourette's, which is a neurological disorder involving repetitive movements or unwanted sounds. Her son was diagnosed and has been in treatment since he was 5 years old. This young student had a very unique type; he sounded like a flock of seagulls.

His first day in class was tough. The fifth grade wing contained four classrooms. His unusual sound could be heard not only in his classroom, but the entire wing. I don't think any of my staff had been prepared for this. The sound could be heard all the way around the turn to the nurse's office.

It so happened that my Association of Learning Consultants

was having a meeting at our school district and we needed a speaker. I called my girlfriend, Dr. Judith Newman, who was a Professor at Penn State Abington. She was elated to help us out. The reason that I called her was her involvement with Tourette's. Her son and nephew were both afflicted with this disorder and Judy was also the president of the Tourette Association of the New Jersey Chapter.

We not only invited our fifth grade teachers and staff, but we included ALC members and interested staff from surrounding districts. The library was packed with teachers and staff who wanted to learn about this rare disorder. Judy gave a wonderful presentation about the types of characteristics that can occur in a child or adult. Some display tics or unusual sounds. Some adults almost bark or curse uncontrollably. Her son Brian had mild symptoms. Judy was a rare find to us just at a time when we needed a workshop. Her time with us served two purposes. She not only educated our teaching staff about this disorder, but her workshop fulfilled our obligation to host other Learning Consultants. This disorder was new to us. We studied it in graduate school, but Judy made it come to life.

Many of Judy's strategies on how to deal with this disorder involved relaxation. My co-worker and school psychologist began thinking of ways to help Jamie. John noticed that the seagull sound only came out of Jamie's mouth when he was stressed. John went to our school nurse and asked her permission to try a strategy out. Her office was down the hall from the fifth grade wing. John gave permission to Jamie to leave the room whenever he got stressed. He would go to the nurse's office and rest in there. The teachers all agreed and were involved in this plan. His mother also agreed to this plan which was a 504 plan due to a medical condition.

To our surprise, the plan worked so well that Jamie's need for respite in the nurse's office became shorter and shorter. It worked so well that Jamie found his own "good." He approached

John and asked if he could give an assembly to the four fifth grade classes. Jamie wanted to give a talk about Tourette's to his fellow classmates and teachers about what it was like living with Tourette's. The day he gave his presentation there wasn't a dry eye in the house amongst his teachers. His classmates asked questions and Jamie answered them honestly. Jamie stood there with pride. He had found his own "good" with the help and guidance of this outstanding school psychologist. John found a strategy that worked after Judy's wonderful speech. I will never forget that day. They say it takes a village to raise children. We all seemed to help each other, but Jamie helped himself!

Adam

It was a quiet Wednesday afternoon after lunch and I was sitting in my office writing a report. A loud voice came over the loudspeaker. "Mrs. Cohen, please report to Room 22 immediately, it's an emergency!"

I ran very quickly and asked the teacher what the emergency was. She replied, "It's a poopie emergency."

"Excuse me, what did you say?"

She said, "Look around the room." There were little balls of poop all over the room. Adam was a third grader in a small self-contained special education class. He was a very round, obese little boy who was also an ELL student. He was from Mexico and spoke very little English.

His teacher was beside herself. She was freaking out. Little balls of poop were falling out of Adam's pants and they were all over the rug in her classroom. She had Adam standing straight up beside her in a total state of frustration. I can honestly say that I have never had a poop emergency. With a high amount of anxiety myself I called our school nurse and asked her to come to Room 22 immediately. She assessed the situation and she said we should have him sent home immediately. An immediate phone call to his mom had to be done immediately to have her come to pick him up. However, we needed to get over one hurdle since his mom spoke no English. Fast thinking occurred, and my school nurse went to the board office down the hall to get our secretary who spoke Spanish to call his mom. My school nurse walked quickly back to her office, retrieved a wheelchair, and swiftly returned with a garbage bag in hand. She wrapped the garbage around Adam and delivered him to his mom at the door in the garbage bag. The evening custodians were called in to clean and fumigate the room.

 I asked our Spanish interpreter to invite mom to a conference in a couple of days after Adam was evaluated by his pediatrician. We needed to know if he had a medical condition. His Mom agreed to come in on Monday afternoon and we booked our Spanish speaking interpreter. Adam had seen his doctor, and his mom came in with paperwork in hand. To our surprise, it was not paperwork from his pediatrician. It was paperwork from C.H.O.P., (Children's Hospital of Philadelphia). In short, it said Adam was diagnosed with Non-Alcoholic Fatty Liver Disease. This is a disease that many adults get when it is related to alcohol consumption. His was due to his extreme overweight condition and the kinds of foods in his main diet.

 We reviewed with Mom what Adam ate each day. Our secretary translator turned white. She reported Mom used lard in each meal that she prepared for Adam to eat. We suggested that she try to have him eat a healthy diet. She looked at us with glazed over eyes and explained that lard is part of their diet. We could watch over Adam's diet while he was in school, but could we change a family's culture? Absolutely not. A teacher has his or her limitations. Unfortunately, we could not find the "good" in Adam.

Sharon Benaderet-Cohen

You cannot solve all of a child's problems, particularly medical ones.

The lesson learned from our experience with Adam, who was an ELL student was to have a meeting with their family in their native language at the beginning of the year. Go over every detail of that student's medical needs. We may have gotten his information in time to prevent a "poopie" emergency and saved that teacher a lot of aggravation.

Charlene

Charlene was beginning fourth grade when her mother requested a meeting with our team. Her teacher joined us to find out more about her new student. Charlene had had a stroke the year before. Her condition was a medical one so we needed to proceed with a 504 plan.

Her academics were fine. Since she was medically involved we met with our school district's 504 chairperson. We filled out the form and indicated Charlene would need to be allowed to go to the nurse at any time if she has a headache.

Conference time came and went, and Charlene received permission to go to the nurse in all subject areas including music, art, library and computers. She received restrictions in gym.

Her teacher let her go to the nurse whenever she had a headache. Her mother was very active in a stroke support group and requested that we have an assembly for all students. This assembly happened during Stroke awareness month and was received quite well by her classmates. Charlene's mother was her greatest advocate. She had found Charlene's "good" and made sure that everything was in place to meet her needs.

Charlene's teacher honored her request to go to the nurse at any time. However, she noted a pattern. Charlene always asked during math. Her teacher noted that her requests came at the same time of day. One day Charlene asked, and her teacher did not honor her request. Needless to say, her mother came in immediately complaining to our school superintendent. Her teacher received negative consequences for not honoring Charlene's request. A teacher may not go against this plan at any time. Her mother continued to find her daughter's "good," yet her teacher was upset that she observed a pattern. Her teacher needed to request a 504 meeting to communicate her observations. Or at the very least, phone home to let her mom know what was going on with her daughter.

Another student I case managed was in middle school. He always walked with a limp arm and hand. I thought he had cerebral palsy. During a conference his mother confided in me that he had had a stroke while in utero. I never knew that was possible. She believed that this was the cause of his learning disabilities. I never observed any true difficulties with him over his years in middle school.

Two years ago I was supervising a student teacher when I was informed that one of her students just had a stroke. He was only in fourth grade. After a six-week absence he returned in a wheelchair. Whenever I observed this student teacher after he returned she was able to do a whole group lesson. Her mentor teacher would sit in the corner with the student in the wheelchair and give him one-on-one instruction. Not only did he come back with physical disabilities, but cognitive delays as well. They were fortunate to have two teachers in the room since she had a student teacher. However, if you're alone you have to schedule accordingly.

Sharon Benaderet-Cohen
Steven

It was a quiet afternoon when a kindergarten teacher walked into my office and said she needed to talk to me about a student. She was quite concerned because he was eating everything in her room. Since this was an informal observation I scheduled my observation the next day during story time. What I observed was totally amazing.

His teacher read a story on the large carpet in the room. Steven sat in his spot picking up pieces of dirt, strings and a variety of tiny objects. After the story, his teacher asked them to go back to their seats and draw a picture of their favorite part. The tables were arranged in clusters with a small plastic container to hold their arts and crafts items. I noticed an empty glue stick and a pencil that had been chewed down to the lead. Also, there were empty crayon papers. Steven had eaten all of these items prior to our visit.

There were school procedures that needed to be followed but since this was an emergency I asked the IR&S Committee to bypass the paperwork. Technically, this teacher needed to bring his name up to this committee which consisted of teachers helping other teachers. They needed to brainstorm ideas and document them for six weeks before a Child Study Team evaluation could take place. My partner John said he thought Steven had Pica. This is a disorder that involves craving and chewing substances that have no nutritional value, such as ice, clay, soil, paper, dirt, or paint.

We called home and had his mother come in to meet with us regarding an evaluation. His mother brought her sister for moral support. We asked our routine questions. John asked if Steven had witnessed any trauma. She replied, "As a matter of fact, Steven witnessed my brother being murdered right in front of me several years ago when he was only three years old." Bingo! Steven had endured one of the most traumatic situations a little boy could endure. His mother gave us permission to test her son to see if he had any delays. He came out on level in all areas including academics and cognitive abilities. We recommended counseling two times per week.

We also recommended that Steven's arts and crafts container be removed from his seat. Whenever he needed these items, the classroom assistant needed to sit by his side to monitor him.

Two years ago I happened to see Steven's teacher at the school's Eighth Grade Graduation. She told me he was in fourth grade and doing fine. I told her that she found Steven's "good."

Her gut instincts were to get help for this little boy immediately. Some of the items he ate were toxic. If she had waited and gone through the process, who knows how many items he would have ingested. This teacher found her student's "good" and helped him get the necessary help immediately. Whenever you have a student who is having a bizarre issue go with your gut instincts. They will never let you down.

Notes

Chapter 11
Equality

We don't choose the students we work with, nor their parents; even if we don't agree with their choice of lifestyle or values, they deserve to be treated with kindness and respect. They need a safe environment and most of all to be treated "equally."

Tonya

Tonya was my most academically challenged student in my MD-Kindergarten. I was prepared to teach kindergarten, but not preschool. Tonya was literally raised in a closet during her first three years of life. Her mother placed her there while she went out to score cocaine. Tonya was born with cocaine addiction. Her nervous system was already challenged. Her way of surviving was to create a language all of her own. She spoke Tonya-ese. The constant gibberish coming out of her mouth made no sense to anyone. She was being raised by her 40-year-old grandmother. She was a very young-looking African-American woman who cared greatly for her granddaughter.

Tonya was a sweet little girl who was raw. She was functioning on a two-year-old level with no language skills. I had to search all over my building for preschool materials to come up with a curriculum to meet her needs. I also supplemented materials from teacher supply stores. Tonya was not equal to her classmates in any way.

I tapped into teaching her academics by singing tunes. I had to think like a two-year-old. The more she heard language from my other students the more she got away from her own made-up language. She remained with me for two years. In that time I found her "good." She learned with the auditory method, singing her way through the alphabet, beginning sounds, and numbers.

I informed her grandmother what strategies were working and she did the same at home. She duplicated everything I did. Tonya sang in speech, occupational therapy, and physical therapy. Everyone tapped into her strength. We all continued to teach to her "good." By the time Tonya left my class two years later she was on a beginner reader level with much improved language skills.

I cannot take full credit. We all acted as a team to address her academic needs. I give the credit to this inspirational grandmother. She was let down raising her daughter and was now doing her grandest to make it up with her granddaughter. This child came to school each day meticulously dressed. Her hair was in braids with colored barrettes. She was clean and well-fed.

This story took place over 30 years ago. A child in my care with significant delays was being raised by her grandmother. Many teachers in present day have students in their classrooms who are being raised by grandmothers. Build positive relationships and give them ways they can help their grandchild. They can be your greatest advocates!

Two Moms

Ty, a tiny African–American three-year-old, was adopted by two women. They came in to meet us to review his need for preschool. He had some academic and language delays. They sat down quietly and introduced themselves as his two moms. We didn't blink. This was over 30 years ago and I'm sure today this might be more common. We treated them with kindness and the respect that they deserved.

Several months went by and Ty was making wonderful progress. They had developed an outstanding relationship with his teacher. Ty's birthday was approaching and his moms requested his teacher place a birthday invitation in each student's book bag. In their generosity they were inviting all of the other seven students to their house on Saturday afternoon.

His teacher contacted me on Monday morning very upset. She said the two moms called her to tell her that not one classmate showed up at Ty's party. I think in those days people were much more judgmental. Little Ty was upset, and his moms were shocked and dismayed. Equality did not exist in those days when two women were raising a little boy.

My best advice is to treat these parents with the same kindness that you would give two parents of the opposite sex. This little boy was devastated for two weeks after his classmates did not come to his party. In this case we had difficulty finding his "good" due to his sadness. He could not figure out why not one of his friends would come to his party. I do not feel in present day the same circumstances would happen. In my heart of hearts I believe people would have more open minds and that two married women would be treated without judgment.

Sharon Benaderet-Cohen

The Man and His Wife

Joey was a very bright little boy. His performance in second grade was exceptional. He excelled in academics and he had exceptional social skills. About halfway into the school year we noticed a drastic difference in his personality. His teacher asked me to join her when she conferenced with his father.

We met one morning at his dad's convenience. To our surprise, in the middle of the conference he began to sob. He said his son's behavior was slumping because of what was happening at home. Joey's mother has left him for her girlfriend. What could you say to that? You need to remain calm, listen, and be compassionate. At least we found out what Joey's problem was. Now we had an understanding of why we couldn't tap into Joey's "good." This could happen in present day. Not all relationships are "equal."

Transgender

Our team was invited to a very confidential meeting in our principal's office. We were getting a new student, but we were sworn to absolute secrecy. Our new fourth grader was a boy for all intensive purposes. His parents confided to us that their son was born a girl, but from a very young age she identified with the opposite sex. They did not even want this information to be given to his teacher.

The first thing we needed to do was to come up with a functional plan. The biggest hurdle we had to get over was to provide a safe environment for bathroom needs. We couldn't send him to the boys room with the other boys. Our fourth graders took two bathroom breaks a day, one in the morning and one in the afternoon. We unanimously decided to send him to the nurse's office to provide a confidential atmosphere. We told his teacher that he had a medical condition and needed the small bathroom. His teacher was never told he was transgendered.

Things went well for the remainder of fourth grade. He developed good peer relationships. His look was a boy's and so were his mannerisms. He identified well with the other boys. Now we were challenged to come up with a plan for fifth grade. The big challenge was that all boys changed in the boys locker room. Could we pull off having him change in the private bathroom in the nurse's office? We did!

These stories disclose that we didn't have to find the "good" in each student and teach to that "good." Our job was to provide equality in their lives. The story of the transgendered boy took place over seven years ago. I'm sure in today's classrooms teachers may be faced with providing a safe environment for a special student. Treat them with dignity, kindness and most of all equality!

Notes

Chapter 12
Confidence

Confidence is a feeling or belief that you can do something well. These two former students displayed confidence in different ways. They were generations apart, yet each displayed an air of confidence and a belief in themselves.

Bonnie

Synchronicity is a concept of "meaningful coincidences" in time. This term has occurred many times in my career. When teaching my multiple disabilities class I was reviewing their IEPs (Individual Education Plans). Many of my students had come from the same preschool handicapped class. While reviewing them I couldn't help notice the signature of their former preschool teacher. This was no coincidence. This had to be the same student who had been in my first fifth grade class.

I decided to call the preschool to speak with her. The secretary was very kind and informed me of a time that I could reach her. When she came to the phone I gave her clues that it was someone from her past. After the first few clues she screamed, "Oh my God, it's Mrs. Cohen." I told her the reason I was calling was to tell her I was teaching her former students. Some people would call this coincidence, but I called it synchronicity.

Bonnie made arrangements to come to my class the following week. I decided not to tell my students. The secretary buzzed her into the school and she made her way to my room. When the door opened, my students were pleasantly surprised. They had no idea that she had been my former student.

She had grown into a beautiful young woman and had followed my chosen career. My principal came into the room and we all posed for a group picture. The heading said, "Mrs. Cohen's students were taught by Mrs. Cohen's student." That was a day I will always remember! Bonnie had found her own "good" and taught herself the skills to become a confident teacher. She seemed so confident interacting with my students. What a strange but wonderful day it was!

We kept in touch for a while and then life happened and we lost touch. Last summer a message popped on my Facebook page. I immediately responded, and we made plans to meet for lunch. Bonnie informed me of the interesting story of how she came to look me up. She is now in her 50s and her 24-year-old son recently injured himself. She took him to Rothman Institute for care. To her surprise, the orthopedic surgeon who cared for him was another former student who had been in her class. Synchronicity once again brought our lives together. She just had to reach me and tell me the "coincidence" that made her get in touch with me again.

Leah

Leah was a student teacher in my first year as a university supervisor at Penn State Abington. She was placed in a wealthy suburban district in Bucks County. She was teaching in a first grade class with an outstanding mentor teacher. I met with both of them at the end of August to develop an overview of the semester. The classroom was already set up. It was a very cheery, inviting classroom.

On my first observation in September, I noticed that Leah was wearing a pair of black three-inch pumps. When I came for the second I noted the same thing. She was still wearing the same high-heeled shoes. During our conference I asked her why she wore such uncomfortable shoes. She looked like they hurt her feet. I told her in teaching she needed to be comfortable and she could wear flats.

She shared with me the method to her madness. All of the teachers in her building wore the same type of shoes. She wanted to fit in, but most of all she wanted a job. If she looked like the teachers and dressed like them she would fit in. During each observation she looked as if her feet continued to hurt. She was trying different ideas to make the pain go away. She persisted each week and never changed her shoes. Guess what happened! She was offered a teaching position in her district in the same grade. Leah had found her own "good" and found her own path to success.

The following year Leah was invited to our end of semester seminar to share her experiences as a first year teacher. She was on a panel with three of our former graduates. While she was sharing her information I looked down at her feet. Leah was wearing flats. She had created her own path and had successfully gotten her dream job! Now she could be at ease with herself and was able to relax and have fun. She had found her own "good." She displayed confidence in herself from her very first day of student teaching. In fact Leah was the most confident student teacher I have ever encountered.

Notes

Chapter 13
Enthusiasm

If you are lucky as a professor, you have enthusiastic students. These two students were exemplary not only in class discussions, but in their participation all the way around. It was a pleasure to work with them. They claim I inspired them; however, my life was touched by them.

Susan

Susan was one of the most enthusiastic students I have ever had at Penn State Abington. She was very actively involved in many activities on campus. To my surprise one week before the end of the semester she came up to me after class. She invited me to the Lion's Ambassadors' Luncheon with the chancellor of the university. Susan was instructed to invite her favorite professor to this luncheon taking place on the last day of class. Needless to say, I was quite flattered.

During the last week of class I highlighted real-world

teaching experiences, including interviews and networking, a most important topic. This could make or break a teacher finding a job. The first directive I gave my student teachers is to go up to the principal during the first week of school, shake their hand firmly, and tell them how fortunate they were to have the opportunity to work in their school for the semester. In teaching it's not so much what you know, but who you know. Making a positive impression makes you more likely to be remembered by that principal. Even if they don't have an opening in their school, they may happen to be friends with another principal who does. In the next to the last class, I shared how my own personal experience with how networking worked in my favor.

When I decided to move from New Jersey to teach in a suburban district in Pennsylvania, I called the director of special education and told him I was interested in teaching in his district. I befriended him and spoke with him every other week. There were no immediate openings, but I continued to call every other week until the end of the school year. In the summer I was set up with an interview and got the job. He told me I did very well and provided excellent answers. There were 1,250 applicants for the job and I got it. I believe it was not so much what I knew, but who I knew. My networking relationship with this director helped me, even though he had no positions when I first contacted him.

After I finished my coursework for my Learning Disabilities Teacher/Consultant certificate, it was time to do my internship. My professor set up my internship at the St. Joseph's Home for Boys in Trenton. My husband and I took a ride to visit it in person. My testing sessions would take place on the third floor. There was a guard on the door, but I still felt unsafe. My role would have been testing 18- to 21-year-old males either on their way to prison or on the way out. This was definitely not the population I wanted to work with.

Touch a Life

In class I expressed my concern to my professor. A girl I was sitting next to mentioned that a particular district in New Jersey was always looking for help. The next day I called and spoke to the director there. After a brief conversation he said, "Come on over." I spent my entire summer in that district testing students and consulting with teachers and parents.

The end of my internship was very near. My director came over to me on the next to the last day. He told me to stand by the coffeepot on my last day. I asked why, and he replied that a director from a neighboring district was coming to meet with him for a meeting at 10 a.m. The next day I was standing by the coffeepot when he offered her a cup of coffee. We struck up a conversation and found out she had a part-time opening. We agreed on an interview the following week and I got the job!

She asked if I wanted to work two days a week or five mornings a week. I chose five mornings so I could get the experience. To my surprise, I got a phone call from my former mentor. She had received a phone call from her friend who was an LD in another district who was overwhelmed with her testing load. They asked me if I would be interested in helping her out. I wound up testing high school students in the afternoons. I made a great salary between the two part-time jobs and I never would have had these opportunities if people hadn't networked with me.

The final networking experience with my LDT/C experience took place after working eight years in my district came after Christmas break. The superintendent in the district where I did my internship had retired. I went to his retirement dinner and found out my former director was taking his place. My former mentor was becoming the director. When I was leaving I asked if there was an opening for an LD. He replied, "Send me your resume."

In June they asked me to come in for an interview. I

interviewed with five other people and got the job. I got the job on my merit, not the fact that I did my internship there. It was a wonderful job for the 13 years I worked there.

It was time to retire after forty-one-and-a-half-years. After one year of lunching with the girls I found myself terribly bored and I wanted to stimulate my brain. Networking took place once again. I was having dinner with my girlfriend who listened to me talk about my boredom. She was a Professor at Penn State Abington where they had an active education department.

I re-invented myself and became an adjunct professor. While teaching my educational theory class the first time, Susan invited me to the Chancellor's luncheon at the beginning of this story. Susan watched firsthand what I meant by networking. I got up out of my seat, shook the chancellor's hand, and introduced myself. As we shook hands, I told her that I was the product of an outstanding Penn State education. I did the same thing with the Dean. After my long career I retired from teaching and was now teaching educational theory at her university. After networking with them they remembered me when I was anywhere on campus. Susan saw me in action and learned the importance of shaking hands firmly with administration and becoming familiar with the administrators and other teachers who may be help you—if not now, at some later time.

I bumped into her after graduation. She told me she began substituting in the district she student taught in. This district was her dream job that she targeted for herself. She was hired to substitute in one school and was guaranteed to work every day. She found her own "good" and networked herself into a long-term substituting position for the second half of the year teaching computers. Way to go Susan!

Kyle

The enthusiasm that exuded from this college sophomore was amazing. His "good" was to move to Japan and become an ESL teacher. This was his dream since beginning college. During each week's sessions he eagerly sat in our class 15 minutes before it began. I would listen to his conversations with the usual girls sitting around him. They engaged in conversations from church services to their goals and aspirations.

Kyle wrote the most detailed reflection papers for my assignments in educational theory. We had gotten up to the poverty section of my syllabus, and I decided to show Diane Sawyer's documentary on Strawberry Mansion High School. This school was considered the most dangerous in Philadelphia. Diane followed the principal, Linda Cliatt, around. She had totally changed the school for the better. This documentary was shown in two parts; it discussed the poverty the students came from. I was a novice professor and I showed part one on my iPad. Kyle politely said, "Mrs. Cohen, you don't need to show it that way. I can show it on the big screen using the Podium." From that day on Kyle was my media go-to person.

During the last day of class I had my students sit in a circle with me. I passed out a paper called "Words to Live By." This paper contained words in a vast array of beautiful colors. The words on this paper have become the Table of Contents in this book. We went around in a circle and each student had to select a word that they would bring into their teaching careers. I started with the word "gratitude." At the end of this exercise, I gave each student a collection of chocolate stars that read, "A Star is Born." To top off my last class I handed each student a personalized note that I had written the night before zeroing in on their unique characteristics.

In today's age of e-mails it's important to have some things permanently written that can be saved. I instructed my students to buy a three-ring notebook and put this positive note in it to save. They were to add to their collection over the years and save other positive notes written by students, parents, and co-workers. Whenever they had a bad day they were to pull out this notebook and read all the positive comments that were written about them. This strategy saved me on many bad days. It's guaranteed to cheer you up again! My student teachers tell me they still have my notes three years later and they thank me for this idea.

During this semester, professors were being in-serviced in sexual harassment. We needed to watch a video about not touching students. I was very careful not to touch any of my male students. They shook my hand on the way out. Kyle grabbed my hand and gave me a huge hug. He whispered in my ear, "Lady, you are phenomenal." Kyle never needed me to find his "good." He was so full of enthusiasm and innately motivated. He was an absolute asset to have in class. Many conversations and debates were struck up in class with this fine young man. I wished him good luck at University Park in the fall and his travels to Japan as an ESL teacher.

Universities need more students like Kyle with their kind, caring demeanors!

Notes

Chapter 14
Inspire

Some student teachers are special because of the odds they overcome. These two student teachers have persisted through intense times but have survived and come out all the better for it. Each of them went through difficult challenges in their own way but they each found their own "good."

Kathryn

Kathryn was my student teacher during my first semester as a supervisor. She was placed in an upwardly mobile school district in a second grade class. The class included two challenging students. One had Oppositional Defiant Disorder (ODD) and the other had Attention Deficit Hyperactivity Disorder (ADHD). Many times when I came to observe her she used proximity control and had each one on either side of her so she could reach them at all times. The student with ODD would eventually shut down, and wound up working with his teacher one-on-one. The student with ADHD was

Touch a Life

a non-stop talker. Kathryn devised a non-verbal communication system that looked like an alligator's mouth closing. This indicated to her student that he needed to stop talking. This signal really worked well.

She had excellent behavior management skills and her lesson plans were well written and executed. Her main problem was her mentor teacher, who was a perfectionist. Kathryn sent me her lesson plans the day before I was to supervise her, so that I could review them. When I arrived the next day to do my observation, Kathryn's cheeks were red. Her mentor teacher changed her lesson plan completely.

Kathryn constantly felt rejected. I would need to try to build her up. It wasn't her fault. It was her mentor teacher's problem. This woman would constantly change things to make things better in her mind.

Kathryn and I met for a debriefing for 30 minutes after I observed her. I spent most of that time building up her self-esteem. She had excellent skills, but constantly felt rejected. We struck up a friendship and she would ask me to share my experiences with her about many topics in education. She soaked up the information. We spoke on many topics and Kathryn absorbed the information readily.

After graduation Kathryn faced more rejection. She developed an outstanding portfolio and began interviewing in many suburban districts. Many interviews ended in more rejections. She watched all of her classmates get jobs. Kathryn spent so much time preparing for these interviews. She became dismayed when one friend just had one interview in August and got the job. Others obtained their positions because they were hired in the same building where they interned.

In late summer Kathryn got a phone call from her principal. She said that she could not offer Kathryn a classroom position, but she did have an offer for her. She could become a one-on-one assistant for an autistic student with more responsibilities teaching small groups. Kathryn took the job thinking it would lead to a permanent classroom position.

Again, more rejection. Every school district she interviewed with told her they were looking for someone with experience. She was perplexed. How could she get experience if they didn't give her an opportunity to work? Now she took things in a different direction. If a job didn't come to her, she would go to the job. A friend of her mother's told her about a school district in Virginia. Kathryn reached out to a handful of principals. She heard from two of them. She interviewed with one principal and when she went back to her room another posting quickly popped up. She received a phone call at 8 o'clock that night. She answered the e-mail and was invited for lunch the next day, along with another principal. She spent two hours with this enthusiastic man. He told her that she was his first round draft pick and hired her on the spot.

Her move to Virginia was destiny. She is teaching a second grade class in this particular school. He told her he wanted someone with a good heart and that everything else would come. The teaching will come, but you can't teach someone to be kind. He stepped out and had two second grade teachers come into the interview to answer any questions. They also told her how great of a man he was and how he was always pro teacher; he would defend you no matter what.

Kathryn found her own "good." Her gut instinct led her to pursue a teaching position in a different locale. Now she is teaching a second grade class with multicultural diversity as well as academic inclusion. These children love her and are quite supportive. The model of this school district pays more attention to the needs of its pupils. Her elementary hours are from 7:30 a.m. to 2:30 p.m. High school begins at 8:30 a.m. Kathryn thinks this district is ahead of Pennsylvania in many ways.

Her school is a "Leader in Me School" teaching the Seven Qualities (habits) of being an effective leader. These are based on Steven Covey's *7 Habits of Highly Effective People.* Their school was recognized as a leader school and all the teachers have leadership. They are the only school in this district. She is in awe of how many students are so respectful and kind to one another.

Kathryn's life has also changed in so many ways. She has been accepted to George Mason University for a Master's of Education degree in Curriculum and Instruction with a Concentration in Teaching Culturally and Linguistically Diverse and Exceptional Learners. Only 16 teachers were selected for this program. She begins in May and will take two years to complete this program. This summer she will work with secondary ELL students.

Kathryn has found her own path in finding her own "good." It took repeated rejections to find her own happy place. She was recently nominated for "Outstanding First Year Teacher of the Year." Kathryn has been such an inspiration to me. She never took those rejections to heart, or took them personally. Her experiences made her even stronger. She persisted until she found her "happy place!"

Ella

Ella was evaluated by her mother's client, who was a doctor, and classified dyslexic. Her cousin was also tested by the same woman. Ella's brother was tested and found gifted/dyslexic with high IQ and B grades. This happened in third grade while in Catholic School. Every time Ella had to do spelling homework, which involved definitions, on Mondays, she had tremendous difficulty. Doing this assignment made her sick to her stomach. She began receiving home instruction and came back to school in December. She was then assigned to Mrs. Madden, a reading specialist, who was certified in the Wilson Method. This method worked well with intense tutoring. She needed to relearn the entire English language. Ella was able to identify the initial and end sounds of a word, but couldn't get the middle sound. Ella was tutored from third to fifth grade. She went to the tutor's house at least two times a week, and three times in the summer. Essentially, she went to school all year round. This tutor gave Ella books to read. It wasn't until eighth grade that Ella actually picked up a book and read it for herself. Her mom read her the first chapter of *Twilight* series. Ella found her own "good" and discovered a passion for reading. From that point on she read the entire *Twilight* series. She was able to do popcorn reading in middle school. Her way of coping with this difficult task was to count the paragraphs, find hers and keep practicing it until it was her turn. She was constantly embarrassed by the mean kids.

By eighth grade she began putting herself into sentences while walking down the hall. This was the beginning of understanding more in science and math. She moved to the middle track for these subjects in high school where she had smaller classes. She received a resource room situation and flourished. It was mid freshman year that her mom asked to have her removed from this class. While growing up, only her best friend knew she had dyslexia. Only one other friend made fun of her. Ella confronted her and straightened her out.

Ella attended Kean University for her first two years of college. She told them she had dyslexia. She needed to supply her IEP or individual education plan. According to this plan she was permitted to have extra time, use a recorder to tape lessons, access to notes that were provided in her text, and use of a computer. Now Ella has definitely found her "highest good" and now reading is her favorite subject. She is proud that it is not her weakness; it's a strength and makes her unique.

When I first met Ella, it was the beginning of my educational theory class, during spring semester at Penn State Abington. She politely stayed after class and showed me her IEP (Individual Education Plan). We looked at the accommodations that needed to be followed and they were the same as Kean University. Ella had these processed through the Learning Center. I needed to sign my copy and she returned them to the Learning Center. I asked Ella if she would mind sharing her story with my students. Dyslexia and learning disabilities were topics I planned to discuss on my syllabus. My class would have more meaning with a real student telling what it is was like to grow up with dyslexia and Ella wanted to share her story.

Ella's goal in life is to become a reading specialist and help students who are like her. Now as a student teacher she is in meetings concerning her young students. She is able to witness her students as they are labeled. Now she is on the other side. She has become a role model for her students. Ella is going to make an outstanding reading specialist because she has lived in their shoes. She is planning to attend Kean University in the fall for her Master's degree. What a marvelous way to give back!

Notes

Chapter 15
Gratitude

There are so many people I am grateful for in my educational journey. These three are the shining examples of those for whom I am truly grateful. They each have touched my life in a very special way. I hope in some small way I have touched theirs.

John Lestino

John was also known as my school husband, partner and co-worker. We worked together as a unit for 13 years. On my first day on the job as an intern learning disabilities teacher/consultant my director told me to go with him to another school to deal with a student with a knife. That was my initiation to working with this man. What I later found out was his kindness and caring for students of all ages.

We did most of our case management together. He was the school psychologist for the district and I was the learning consultant. Much of our case management overlapped. He worked with students with behavior problems and my students had academic difficulties. In most cases we attended each other's meetings together.

Spending so much time together you become like a sister and brother. Some of our students really believed John was my husband. Some days we spent extra hours testing students in order to get our report into the hands of parents by the deadline. We would complete it by 6 p.m. and deliver it to their mailbox. It was those times that I was able to witness his brilliant mind and tremendous insight into the child's brain. John would get up each morning at 4 a.m. just to read the latest brain research and it showed in his reports.

John had a boy's group for the sixth grade boys. They brought their lunches into his office to eat together and talk. They shared their experiences on many different topics. Most of all, he taught them the skills of how to be a good man. John demonstrated how to develop into a positive human being. Those boys really loved those talks and I don't know anyone who could do it better. He displayed excellent citizenship models. I became an "honorary boy" and was invited to several lunches. My favorite was when they taught me football right before the Super Bowl. They would teach me how to watch for passes, throws, and touchdowns. I would come back after the game to report what I observed in the game. What a thrill it was in watching those boys evolve over a year from little boys to young men. It was all due to their leader, John Lestino.

The day I was most proud of John was when he returned from Louisiana during a school psychologist's convention. John received the honor of being "School Psychologist of the Year" in the nation, not just New Jersey, in 2008. This was after the year of Katrina, the largest hurricane to hit Louisiana. Our team was so proud of him and asked questions about the ceremony where all of his friends and family watched. John's replied, with tears in his eyes, "It was great that my wife and family got to watch me accept this prestigious award. However, the highlight of his week was helping rebuild a playground at an elementary school." This man has so much caring, compassion, and kindness for students. He is a genuine light who helps the students succeed. He is known to all students in the district, not just those he personally worked with. I am fortunate to have had the opportunity to work with this fine educator. John touched the lives of all students he worked with and they in turn touched his life in a positive way!

Dr. Kathy Fadigan

Dr. Fadigan was in charge of the education department at Penn State Abington in 2014. I have great gratitude for her believing in me. After two interviews, each lasting an hour and a half, she called me very late one Friday afternoon. She explained that they did want to hire me; however, they didn't have this particular class in educational theory: multicultural perspectives. After asking if I would be interested in writing the course, she told me that they wanted a real teacher to teach the course. I had never written a college course level before, but I had the varied teaching experiences to pull from.

After four months I had the finished product that needed to be approved by University Park. Once the approval came I had to write the syllabus. I knew which headings I wanted to make this course meaningful for my students. The topics I chose included: building positive relationships with students and parents and co-workers; ethnic, cultural and linguistic diversity; poverty; providing an inclusive environment; and classroom environments.

Next, I needed to find several books to use for supporting my content. The most difficult task was finding articles to support my content. It took four hours in the library sitting with a most patient librarian teaching me the database to find articles for my reflection assignments. All had to be approved by Dr. Fadigan.

I taught the course for several semesters. Never in my wildest dreams did I think being an adjunct professor could be so much fun. In order to make my class interesting, I decided to share three different stories of past students. To this day I have students stop me on campus thanking me for those stories. They made me smile because they remember the details so well. They loved my class because I made it real. Kathy once stopped in to observe me when I was telling a story of a three-year-old who had eaten its parakeet's head. Yes, we had to evaluate this youngster in his home, not knowing what to expect. She was quite taken back, just as we were in the situation.

Penn State didn't want a professor in this course to merely assign chapters in a book. I knew I exceeded their expectations when I received critiques by my students. These stories are how my book *Touch a Life* was born. This book is a collection of those inspirational stories of how students touched my life and how I touched theirs. Teaching is an art, but it takes a very special educator to find the "good" in their student and teach to that "good."

Our campus was exploding in the education department. There was now a need to hire a part-time supervisor of student teachers. After interviewing with Dr. Fadigan and the director of student teachers for a new position, I got the job. My new duties included observing student teachers in the field. I got to share my 41 years in education and my expertise with these 22-year-old seniors. I shared my stories with them during our seminars. At times they stared at me questioning my varied student experiences. At the end of this semester I give them a personalized note that ends with: "Always remember you have the power to touch a life!"

Dana

My daughter Dana did fairly well in elementary school. Things did not get difficult for her until fifth or sixth grade. Her teachers informed me that she did not perform well in tests so they recommended her for the next to the lowest level group in middle school. She had average intelligence, but she wasn't able to perform well on standardized tests. This placement was devastating to her in many ways.

While in high school, a guidance counselor told her if she was going to college it would only be a community college. In this counselor's opinion a four-year college was out of the question. As an educator I questioned how this woman could impede her limiting beliefs on my daughter.

Dana was accepted at a Penn State campus that offered a Provisional program. This program was designated for students who were weak in their skills. Shortly after the beginning of the semester I received a phone call from the woman who was in charge of Dana's program. She suspected that Dana had a learning disability and wanted to test her using the Woodcock-Johnson III. A fee would've been $500.00. I informed her that's what I did for a living and that I charged the same thing. As her parent I suspected that Dana had an auditory processing deficit. For example, when given directions orally, Dana had difficulty processing them. She needed a visual to go with them.

We then discussed what accommodations could be given to Dana without formal testing. Since she was in the Provisional program she was permitted to use a tape recorder to record lessons and have extra time on tests. Since we knew these were the same accommodations she could receive without classification we decided not to have her formally tested. They also recommended that she take fewer credits each semester. I was so thankful to this

Sharon Benaderet-Cohen

woman and this program because they gave Dana an excellent start in her educational journey.

After one year in this program Dana transferred to Penn State Abington. It was there that she actually discovered a love for learning. It took her six years to complete a four-year degree. She graduated with a degree in Psychological/Social Sciences.

Upon graduation Dana decided to pursue a degree as a sex therapist. She searched for a graduate school that offered this program and she found Widner University. After five years she received a degree in Human Sexuality; however, she did not receive a license to go with the degree. This was a brand new program and they still had not gotten the kinks out yet.

My daughter had a new choice to make. Either go for a Ph.D. or a second Master's degree. She did not want to spend the next five years of her life in graduate school so she chose the second Master's. She was accepted at Lasalle and completed a program in Marriage and Family Counseling. Her graduation day was truly miraculous. I am so grateful to her for showing me persistence and fortitude. From that first week in school, she never gave up. I admire her courage to not believe in any labels. She just knew in her heart that she needed to learn differently and work at a slower pace. Yet she achieved such heights. She had found her own "good."

Upon graduation she began looking for a job. She wound up getting a job in the admissions department of a drug and alcohol rehab. After five years she knew she needed a change. She wrote a three-page proposal and handed it into the CEO and said we really need this position here. He offered her the job and she began work in the Family Services Department. When a person comes into the rehab and goes to detox, she works with their families. By taking the initiative she created her own "good."

Several years ago my daughters and I served on Dr. Judy

Newman's Ethics class on campus. At the end of the panel she encouraged her students to come up at the end and speak with the panel if they had any questions. A young man came up and firmly shook my daughter's hand and said, "You may not remember me but it is because of you that I am clean and sober today. You also helped my mom. Now I am going to graduate school to become a Clinical Psychologist." I got goose bumps. My daughter had touched someone's life! I am so grateful for having this beautiful girl in my life. She has taught me true courage and I am forever grateful for her. She is presently branching out and is now doing private therapy with families. She is fulfilling her passion and her purpose in life. I could not be prouder!

    I share her story on purpose. Many times in my career I had parents who were hesitant to label their students in high school. I would encourage them to do whatever they could to get the best services they could. My daughter's story is encouraging to a young population. She went onto greatness and never looked back with any negativity. I am so proud to call her my daughter and I am filled with gratitude!

Notes

Chapter 16
Win-Win

    A lesson I have learned throughout my career in education is to make everything a win-win situation. Many meetings can be solved with a win-win with a parent, student, or co-worker. I always tried to make wonderful agreements that were fair so that all should come out a winner. This philosophy got me through many tough meetings. I always shook hands with the parent in the beginning of the meeting and let them know how we were all working to make it a win-win for their child. This habit made me quite successful with everyone!

    At the beginning of my teaching career I discovered the importance of a win-win situation. When I started teaching in 1972, the curriculum in New Jersey included teaching gym. Yes, teachers were required to teach physical education because we did not have gym teachers. I always had a talent for arts and crafts, but I never liked gym when I had it in high school and college. Now I had to teach my fifth grade class a half hour of gym a day.

I became friendly with another fifth grade teacher in my wing. She was a jock and loved to play volleyball, softball and other games. We came to an agreement very quickly. We decided to share activities, since we shared the same gym time each day. She supervised and I helped. During major art activities I supervised, and she helped. That was my first experience developing a win-win for each teacher. We each used our talent and skills and shared them for the betterment of our students.

The next time I developed the strategy of win-win was when I taught my first special education class when I had Luke, the student who was beyond ADHD. The Learning Consultant I worked with wanted me to give him three red stickers every five minutes. I asked if I could develop a board game so he could obtain stickers for each subject. We had a win-win that allowed me to deliver rewards to him that were more meaningful for me.

Luke's mother sent me notes every day on where she was going to shop that morning. The notes were extremely detailed. She did this because she was afraid her son would be injured. I could've asked her to stop the notes and embarrass her; instead, I made it a win-win for both of us. Each day I put the notes in a file and she kept sending them. No negative comments needed to be said.

While teaching in that same class, I made a win-win with my principal. She was a former reading specialist with no special education background. During an observation she actually took the chalk out of my hand and tried giving my students a three-step direction. I did not want to oppose her when I knew my students could not do that. In my head I decided to make it a win-win situation for both of us. I thanked her and said I would try that strategy for the next two weeks and let her know how it went. I never had to challenge her in a negative way. I actually created a neutral designation for both of us.

Touch a Life

My career as a Learning Disabilities Teacher/Consultant was a natural for creating win-win situations for everything I did. My position on a child study team was working with a teacher and principal to create the best situation for a student. I never went into a meeting without the thought of developing a win-win plan. We were a triangle together. I always started a meeting with positive comments about a student.

I worked with many divorced, or separated parents. Instead of having a negative, nonproductive meeting with both parents together, I learned to accommodate each one. I had a separate meeting for each parent and developed a win-win for each.

It's extremely important to know which parent has custody. I encouraged my teachers to go to the file in the office and see which parent has custody, and to never release the student to the wrong parent. This created a win-win for all of us.

The lessons I learned in working closely with principals, teachers, and students created my idea for creating win-wins. I learned through making mistakes and tried to pass my knowledge to the teachers and student teachers I have worked with. It makes your meetings more positive and everyone a winner.

Notes

Conclusion
I Can Do It!

Reflecting on how I got here took some time. I've always had an "I Can Do It" personality. From that first peek into a room full of challenging students I developed my love and passion for working with difficult students. This book is full of the many experiences I have had in my extensive career. Many times I have heard from administrators, "We are giving you this student because of your kind, loving personality." My answer to them was, "You picked the right educator. I know I can figure this child out and succeed with him."

Today I have turned to my magical purple notebook. Every time I have received a positive note from a student, parent, co-worker, or administrator I put the note into the notebook. After 44 years I have quite a collection. This is a tool that I give my interns and student teachers. They always start off their collections with my positive note about them. Then when they are having a really bad day, they can open their notebook and see what great skills they have.

My notebook has brought me to the end of this part of my journey. This tool has shown me all of the positive reflections from so many people. For example, I found an article from my first communications handicapped class that was published in the *Burlington Times*. My class studied butterflies. They thought they were learning science, but I was teaching them an appreciation and awareness for life.

Testimonials from parents include thanking me for being a major influence guiding a son for five impressionable years. That mom told me I made a great difference and that I treated her son calmly and lovingly. "You've been a constant support and a positive attitude to help him develop a good self-image. If all teachers cared about their pupils as much as you have we'd have fewer problems in the world and more well-adjusted adults."

Another parent note thanked me for my help, support and guidance. She also mentioned that I gave her encouragement, reassurance, and hope. "People like you pour their heart and soul into what they do and you've made a difference in my son's life. He's growing and learning beyond our wildest dreams."

A collection of remarks from administrators include, "...patience, concern and caring, dedicated to the well-being of each and every child with whom she has contact. Sharon is a strong child advocate and master teacher. She is a strong educator with a high degree of professionalism. She has excellent instructional skills and a varied repertoire of strategies designed to meet the needs of special education children. Mrs. Cohen is a rare individual who combines expertise with the art of teaching."

Yes, this is certainly a testimonial to my strengths as an educator. My secret—to be determined to never fail! I learned from a special principal, Hattie Green. Whenever I talked about my students I referred to them as special education students. She turned to me one day and said, "Students should not be labeled. They are just children. You need to teach to the child." From that point on I shot to the stars! I focused on what they could do and not what they couldn't. My passion continued in each and every educational experience I had. Embrace each child's uniqueness and go from there. They are special and unique in some way. Find that way and you can discover your own passion in working with them.

In closing, I'd like to quote the *Daily News,* May of 1987. My family attended a tribute to the songwriter, Linda Creed. I was interviewed after Whitney Houston sang *The Greatest Love of All.* We adopted this song as our class song. As this song says, "I believe the children are our future, teach them well and let them lead the way." This was my formula for success that led to my passion and excitement for education.

Find the "good" in a student and teach to that "good." It makes everyone a WINNER!

Acknowledgments

I dedicate this book to my wonderful husband of 46 years. He has supported me during my 44-year career in education. When I got my first job in 1972 after graduating from Penn State University, he became part of my class. When a student was hospitalized, he joined me in my visit. He then supported me through earning my Master's Degree in Special Education. Most of the childcare for my two daughters, who were six and eight, fell on him since I spent my days working and nights studying. When I got my first special education job, he became my cheerleader. He came to concerts, plays, school fairs, and fashion shows. In my most recent position as a learning consultant, he became an honorary member of the faculty, attending school concerts and plays as well as faculty functions. He even attended the wedding of one of our Interns.

I would also like to thank my editor, Karen Hodges Miller, for her continued support. Many special thanks to Eric Labacz for the beautiful covers he designed.

About the Author

    Sharon Benaderet-Cohen began her 44-year career in education at Penn State University, majoring in elementary education. After teaching fifth grade for three years, she realized her calling and passion was special education. She received a Master's degree in Special Education and taught in many different types of classes for 17 years. These included: Communication Handicapped, Multiple Disabled, Learning Disabled, and Emotionally Disturbed.

    After 20 years of teaching, she changed her career and once again attended the College of New Jersey, receiving a certification as a Learning Disabilities Teacher/Consultant. She spent 21 years assessing students for various disabilities including learning difficulties and autism. She also case managed them after placing them in an appropriate program. Some students were followed from two and a half to eighth grade. A Supervision Certificate followed which allowed her to become an Adjunct Professor at Rowan University in New Jersey supervising interns who were becoming LDT/C's. Her vast 41-year career ended in retirement after she touched the lives of many students as well as their families.

Sharon Benaderet-Cohen

Most recently she re-invented herself as an adjunct professor at Penn State University at Abington Campus. She was asked to write the Educational Theory/Multiple Perspectives class based on her varied teaching experiences. In addition to teaching this class, she has also supervised student teachers in the field, sharing her experiences in teaching. She felt that she was giving back to her full circle of education, sharing her knowledge with her student teachers.

Her career has finally come full circle. Utilizing her knowledge of the art of teaching along with the many successes she has had, she was inspired by her students to write a book, *Touch a Life,* a collection of inspirational stories of finding the "good" in a student and teaching to that "good." This passion has been her mantra—when you inspire a student, they, in turn, inspire you to be a better teacher!

Sharon is presently focusing on a speaking career for professional development days in school districts, colleges, and universities as well as Parent Teacher Organizations.

Made in the
USA
Middletown, DE

74706057R00076